# EMPLOYMENTOLOGY

Jing,
Chase your Passion, not your Pension! Darnell

## A Practical Systematic Methodology

## of

## Finding Employment

## by a

## Hiring Manager

---

Darnell Clarke

**http://www.darnellclarke.com**

First Printing April, 2012



**Disclaimer**

The information published in this book represents the opinions, personal research, and business experience of the author. Since the success of anyone depends upon the skill and ability of the person, the author makes no guarantees and disclaims any personal loss or liabilities that may occur as a result of the use of the information contain herein.

This publication is designed to provide accurate and authoritative information in regard to the subject matter covered in it. It is provided with the understanding that the publisher is not engaged in rendering legal, accounting, or other professional services. If legal advice or other expert assistance is required, the services of a competent professional person should be sought.

ISBN: 978-0-9854041-0-9
ISBN-10: 0985404108

The Clarke Group

## Dedication

To my wife and best friend Cecile, I dedicate this book to you for always believing in me no matter how many jobs I left in the pursuit of happiness. I thank God for letting me find you!

## Acknowledgments

I want to acknowledge and thank Trina Hill, who collaborated with me and gave me the idea and motivation to write this book. Also I thank Greg & Keysha Bradley for taking time out of their busy schedules to do the initial editing. May God Bless you and keep you all your days.

# Table of Contents

Chapter One

# MY STORY

*I am an expert at finding and obtaining employment*

I have had an unusual career path. My journey has taken me from being an ex-major league professional baseball player, to leading the efforts for the Atlanta Olympic Games, to working and consulting with and for some of the largest companies in the world, to building and running a small information technology (IT) business. My academic credentials include two degrees; a MBA and a BA in Computer Science. Throughout my career, my most important asset has been my ability and proficiency to always find employment.

Over the past 20 years, I have worked for 16 companies, in my last 10 positions my salaries were in excess of over $100k each. **I am an EXPERT at finding and obtaining employment**! If you have a tooth problem you go to a dentist, if you have a legal problem you go to a lawyer; if you want to know how to find employment, you must go to someone who is an expert at getting employed.

You go to someone who has actually searched and found employment over and over and over again.

The reason why I have had so many jobs in my career is because I did not know my passion, my calling, my purpose, my chief aim in life. Because of this, I went from job to job chasing the "all mighty dollar." And I was very successful at doing that. My plight is now your benefit.

Over those 20 years, I have submitted over 5000 resumes, I have taken over 300 phone and/or face-to-face interviews. On the flip side, I am a practitioner; I am NOT a recruiter, a headhunter or Human Resource (HR). I am a hiring manager working for a global fortune 100 company; I have given over 200 interviews and have hired over 150 people in my career. So I know what hiring managers are looking for and what they are not. It all starts with your resume.

So the question is: Have I used this *EMPLOYMENTOLOGY* process recently? The answer is a resounding "YES". In March of 2010, I temporarily relocated from Atlanta to Detroit to work for a company. My plan was to move my entire family from Georgia to Michigan. But in October of that year, I decided not to relocate my family and I moved back to Georgia in November 2010. In the second week of November 2010, the week before Thanksgiving, I began my job search using the *EMPLOYMENTOLOGY* process.

Within two weeks of submitting my resumes, I received three (3) phone calls from interested companies, which resulted into two (2) in-person face-to-face interviews for the month of November. During the month of December, I received four (4) more phone calls from interested companies, which resulted into three (3) more in-person face-to-face interviews.

Then everything shut down for the Christmas Holidays. For three weeks during the holidays I submitted over 40 resumes. Contrary to popular belief, companies do hire during the Christmas holiday season. Moreover, three (3) more companies scheduled me for in-person interviews for the first week of January, 2011. During the month of January 2011, I went on six (6) in-person interview, and I accepted a verbal committed offer from a reputable firm on January 31, 2011. I received the formal written offer for employment from the same firm on February 3, 2011 and began working there on February 14, 2011 and I am still employed there as of the writing of this book.

From the second week of November 2010, until I accepted an employment offer on February 3, 2011, I submitted over 160 resumes to actual open positions via company websites. Those 160 plus submitted resumes resulted into a total of twenty (20) phone and/or in-person face-to-face interviews. Lastly, out of those 20 interviews I was offered 3 positions, I declined two and accepted one. See *Appendix C* for complete list of those 20 companies I interviewed with during that time period. **I am an <u>EXPERT</u> at finding and obtaining employment.** Now let me explain how *you* can become an expert too... LET'S GET STARTED!

Chapter Two

# Unemployment is Inevitable

*The person who gets the job is not the most qualified for the job; it's the person who is the most qualified at getting the job.*

Let's get one thing straight, unemployment is inevitable! Gone are times when you work for one employer 10, 15, 20 years or more. Those days are gone forever and will not come back in our lifetime. So get used to being unemployed. The fact is you will get fired, laid-off, down-sized, or riffed (*meaning to have dismissed an employee because their job was eliminated*) sometime in your career. Get used to it! Remaining employed oftentimes has nothing to do with you; it has to do with the well-being of the company itself. Your company can be great today and out of business tomorrow. This is why you will need to become an expert at finding and obtaining employment, over and over again. That's what I have become. **I am an EXPERT at finding and obtaining employment**!

Back in the early 2000's, many companies were looking for warm bodies. All you had to do was put your resume out there or talk to a few recruiters and the offers started rolling in. Not anymore. We were once in a candidate driven market. Today, it's employer driven. Many companies are not posting their openings to job posting boards because the responses are too overwhelming, and time consuming to process and too costly.

Employers receive thousands of resumes with only one or two that are compatible for the open position(s). A lot of companies have experienced major layoffs. They have not advertised those jobs because the downsizing allowed them the ability to "take out the trash". In other words, getting rid of the under qualified, over compensated people they were pretty much forced to hire the last couple of years. To be politically correct, companies cannot lay-off someone citing restructuring or lack of work (skill/ethic) and then turn around and post that job!

Remember this statement: "***The person who gets the job is not the most qualified for the job; it's the person who is the most qualified at getting the job***". Meaning, if you want to get employed, you must become an expert at finding and obtaining employment. You must be relentless, persistent and unyielding. You must be committed! Until you are committed, there is hesitancy; a chance for you to draw-back. Allow me to say this right now, the reason most people are still unemployed after nine months to a year of seeking employment is for several reasons. The first reason is they fail to use a systematic approach to find employment and they don't use a methodology. A *methodology* is generally a guideline for solving a problem by using a particular discipline. The second reason is, people submit resumes to job openings they are not qualified for, be it experience, training, education, etc. This job searching thing is a numbers game. You have to find the companies that have open job opportunities and submit your resume to that opening, and you have to do it over and over, day after day, week after week, month after month; in some cases year after year. You cannot ever stop until you get that job. It is that simple. Not easy but that simple.

At the time of writing this book, according to the U.S. Bureau of Labor Statistics, in 2011, employment growth averaged 137,000 per month. There were (13.1 million) unemployed persons and the unemployment rate was (8.5 percent) in December, 2011.

Among the major worker groups, the unemployment rate for adult men decreased to 8.0 percent in December, 2011. The jobless rates for adult women (7.9 percent), teenagers (23.1 percent), whites (7.5 percent), blacks (15.8 percent), and Hispanics (11.0 percent) showed little change. The jobless rate for Asians was 6.8 percent.

Private-sector job gains totaled 212,000 in December, 2011 and 1.9 million over the year. Employment in transportation and warehousing rose by 50,000 in December, 2011. The couriers and messengers industry accounted for almost all of the gain (+42,000), as seasonal hiring was particularly strong in December, 2011. This may reflect increased online purchasing during the holiday season. Retail trade continued to add jobs in December (+28,000), with increases in both general merchandise and clothing stores. Retail trade employment has increased by 240,000 over the past 12 months. Manufacturing employment rose in December (+23,000); all of the increase occurred in durable goods manufacturing. In 2011, manufacturing job gains totaled 225,000. Employment in mining continued to increase in December (+7,000). Over the year, mining employment rose by 89,000.

Health care employment continued to expand in December (+23,000). The industry added 315,000 jobs in 2011. Over the month, job gains continued in hospitals (+10,000). Employment in food services and drinking places continued to trend up in December (+24,000). Employment in the industry rose by 230,000 in 2011. Employment in government changed little over the month. This sector lost 280,000 jobs over the year with declines in local government; state government, excluding education; and the U.S. Postal Service.

Since December 2007, at the beginning of the recession, the unemployment rate has risen from 4.9 percent to 8.5 percent in December 2011—the highest rate since the early 1980s. On the basis of the labor force projections and a target Gross domestic product (GDP) growth rate, the economy is expected to be at full employment with unemployment rate of 5.1 percent in 2018.

I'm here to tell you that you don't have to be in those numbers. Companies are hiring all the time. In December, 2011 alone, more than 140,000 jobs were created. <u>*You*</u> could be one of those that find a job. I have created a practical systematic methodology for finding and obtaining employment. I have used this approach for finding employment for over 20 years. I don't know anyone who has been more successful in finding and obtaining employment than me. **I am an EXPERT at finding and obtaining employment**!

You may be asking questions like "what companies are hiring?" Where do you find those companies? How do I submit my resume for actual open positions? I call this book EMPLOYMENTOLOGY for a reason. An <u>-OLOGY</u> is a discipline of study, basically it means "the study of something or of a particular subject". This book was created from over 20 years of me finding employment over and over again. This book discusses finding and obtaining employment from a hiring manager's perspective using the internet. Why? Because many companies have a very small HR (Human Resource) department and they use the internet to post and receive resumes for current and future career opportunities. Most companies are no longer using job posting boards to post open positions because the cost can be substantial. For each posting to one of these job posting boards, it cost a company around $5,000 - $15,000 per posting.

Moreover, 90% of the unemployed are focused on these job posting boards, so companies are inundated with resumes. If you submit your resume to these posting boards, you could be competing against more than 200 other candidates per job listing. You don't stand a chance of getting your resume noticed.

By focusing on actual individual companies and not on internet job posting boards, *EMPLOYMENTOLOGY* provides a process for finding companies. This methodology is NOT jazzy and it may not seem appealing; it's just a step-by-step methodical way of finding employment. This guide addresses finding those companies with open job positions so you can submit your resume. Period! Remember, if you don't submit your resume you won't get an interview and without an interview; you will have no chance at getting employed. Submitting your resume is your number one objective - this is a numbers game. The more resumes you submit, the more chances you have to be selected for an interview.

Your resume serves only one purpose and that is to get you an interview!

Chapter Three

# Historical Job Seeking Techniques

*Searching for a job can really suck if you constrain yourself to the typical tools*

Searching for a job can really suck if you constrain yourself to the typical tools such as online jobs boards, trade publications, Craigslist and networking with only your close friends. You are probably running into the same problems that everyone who is job searching is having. You've posted your resume on all the job boards. You've responded to hundreds of jobs. You're getting nowhere but tired and frustrated. Posting your resume and responding to jobs on job posting boards WILL NOT GET YOU AN INTERVIEW! Things have changed. There are thousands of qualified candidates in the market right now. Competition is stiff. Companies are only looking for someone who has been there, done that.

Now is NOT the time to stretch your wings or try to transfer your skills. Look at your resume objectively or have someone else do it. What are your key strengths? If you've spent twelve years in Storage and two at an Internet start-up, guess what? It's time to look for a job in Storage. You may also want to forgo any increase in salary or title that you attained in the last 18 months. Get lean and mean. In these kinds of times, you need to use every weapon you can and one many people don't or at least don't use to the fullest extent and which is individual company's websites.

Currently, most people attempt to find employment by creating a profile and searching on one of the many internet job-posting websites. Below are a few of the well-known websites:

**CareerBuilder -** www.CareerBuilder.com
**Indeed -** www.Indeed.com
**SimplyHired -** www.SimplyHired.com
**LinkedIn -** www.LinkedIn.com
**Monster -** www.Monster.com
**USAJobs -** www.USAJobs.com government job site
**Yahoo HotJobs -** www.hotjobs.yahoo.com
**TheLadders -** www.theladders.com (cost to access)
**Hound -** www.Hound.com $$$ (cost to access)

Some sites, like The Ladders and Hound make you pay to take advantage of their so called high-paying job services. Never and I mean NEVER pay for any internet job posting websites! Moreover, never pay for any resume or cover letter writing services. You can write just as well as the so called experts. For these experts to write your resume and cover letter, they have to ask you for all the necessary content which includes your background, skills and qualifications. They then take your information and simply reformat it into something that looks nice. You can do that!

Trust me when I tell you I have made every mistake when it comes to finding employment. I have paid hundreds of dollars to those so-called experts over my career to write my resume & cover letter and not once did I receive a job offer using the traditional approach. As a matter of fact, I never received a single interview. I also paid hundreds of dollars to executive recruiters, headhunters, and job posting websites (i.e. The Ladders & Hound) as well. I never received one interview for all the money I spent with those so-called experts; therefore, never pay anyone for things you can do yourself.

Most people waste their time creating profiles and searching the above types of job posting websites and having little to no success in ever getting a phone call from a prospective employer. So, the question is why? There are two problems:

**Problem #1: Searching public sites vs. individual company sites**

People are still looking for employment the same way they did 10 years ago. In the late 1990's and early 2000's the way people got jobs was to search job positing website boards, because that's how companies posted their openings. Then those companies would sit back and wait for all the resumes to come pouring in. The issue was those companies were inundated with resumes from candidates that did not qualify for those postings.

When you respond to jobs listed on posting boards, your resume ends up in a black hole, a passive database most times. If you are responding to the job right from the board, it's going to HR. Bad move. These guys are up to their eyeballs and usually don't even really know what the hiring manager is looking for. That is, if the HR person even sees the resume (again, the passive database). You need to get to the hiring manager, not HR. How? By going to the job posting board and searching for a job that looks like it's a fit. Did you notice I didn't say to search for one that looks interesting? You must go to that company's website and submit your resume on their site. I strongly recommend you do this because, somewhere around 2005, companies started creating their own career job posting websites and stopped using the public internet job posting boards for their open positions.

**Problem #2: Out dated information on public sites**

Since the majority of companies now are using their own career posting websites, there are less open positions listed on the internet public job positing websites. Case in point, you will find the same job postings on CareerBuilder, Monster, Indeed and SimplyHired.

Once you have searched one, you really have searched them all. Sometimes you will find different open positions on the internet public job positing websites, but not often. Also, you will find their postings are NOT current. Many times during a search, I have found a posting that read something like “6 days ago”, meaning this open position was posted 6 days ago.

I would then go to that actual employers website to find that open job on their career posting site, only to find that position was really posted 3, 4, or 5 weeks ago and that posting is no longer available; meaning its closed and/or filled already. In other words, if I would have submitted my resume for that position, my resume would have been automatically deleted or discarded, which is a waste of my valuable time and effort.

Chapter Four

# NEW JOB SEEKING TECHNIQUES

*Chase your passion not a pension*

As of this writing, unemployment is beginning to slowly come down. More companies are starting to hire, so this is your golden opportunity to find the "Job of your Dreams". I'm going to give you the avenue to pursue that dream. Below are the short versions of the 7 action steps that will help you find employment. I have gone one step further, by breaking each of these steps down and providing you detailed instructions on how to use them to get employed. If you follow these 7 steps, I promise you, you will find the job that you are desperately seeking.

***Step 1: Find your Passion***

One of the seeds to success is finding your Purpose, your Passion, and your Chief Aim in Life. This means you are to seek and find your Passion. Chase your passion not your pension. If you do this before anything else, I guarantee you will be in the top 5% of all Americans.

***Step 2: Creating your Resume***

Write your own resume in MS Word and TEXT format. Some companies require you to copy and paste your resume into their career posting website and your resume will keep its format when you copy and paste it from a TEXT file instead of MS Word.

***Step 3: Create Company List***

Creating a short and giant master list of companies you would like to work for that fits your skill-set or qualifications by capturing each firm's career job posting website URL link.

***Step 4: The Job Search***

Start your job search first by traversing through the **Short List** then pursue the **Giant Master List** of Companies. Every Monday morning start with the first company on your short list and don't stop until you check every career website on that list. You should continue to go through your giant master list of companies Tuesday thru Friday. You must check every company on your master list. You must do this each week without fail.

***Step 5: Create your Profile***

Each time you find an opening at a company's website, make sure you create your own personal profile to capture your personal information, resume, cover letter, user id and password.

***Step 6: Networking***

Get the word out. Tell everyone you know that you're looking for a new position because a job search these days requires the "*law of large numbers*". Tell everyone you know because the job they interviewed for last week and didn't get just might be your new job! There is no shame in seeking a job. The more people who know you're looking the more likely you are to find a job.

***Step 7: Interviewing that will get you employed***

*The person who gets the job is not the most qualified for the job; it's the person who is the most qualified at getting a job.* If you don't remember anything else, remember that quote! Your resume was created and submitted for only one reason; TO GET AN INTERVIEW! Interviewing is addressing one question and that is; "What can you do for me"? What "Value Added Proposition" (VAP) can you bring to an organization that will help solve a business problem? This is the 'bottom line' question that all employers want YOU to answer. The better you can answer this question the better chance you will get hired. You must be in the problem solving business. Everything you do and say in the interview must address this VAP question.

To assure your understanding and success, each step has been broken down into greater detail, so you can use them to your advantage in finding and obtaining your dream job.

Chapter Five

# YOUR SEVEN ACTION STEPS

*Get in the zone and stay there – Find out what you do well and keep on doing it. Don't ask what I'm doing right; ask what am I doing WELL?*

Before I get started, let me give you one of the seeds to the secret of success. There is no one secret to success. Instead, there are many seeds which will produce success.

**Step 1: Find your Purpose, Passion, Chief Aim in Life** One of the seeds to success is finding your Purpose, your Passion and your Chief Aim in Life. If you do this first before anything else, I guarantee you will be in the top 5% of all Americans who enjoy a successful life. Allow me to share with you my definition of success. Success is not defined as how much material wealth you have or how much money you can acquire, success is defined as: "The progressive realization of a worthy goal." You are to do this by living successfully *one day at a time!*

You are to do "each" day, all that can be done that day. You don't need to overwork or to rush blindly into your work trying to do the greatest number of things in the shortest possible amount of time. Don't try to do tomorrow's or next week's work today.

Your success in life will be largely determined by your ability to find your true calling. You must work to find the right work for you to do, and you must put your whole heart into doing it in an excellent fashion. You were put here on the earth for a reason. It is up to you to seek and find that reason or your true calling. You will only be truly happy when you discover what you were meant to do. That's success for me!

Successful people move on their own initiative, but they know where they are going before they start. This is called "Definiteness of Purpose"; a specific objective toward which you are working. Successful people don't settle for anything short of what they set out to get. You can write your own success story if you find your own definiteness of purpose. The first factor is this: The first starting point of ALL achievements is the adoption of a definiteness of purpose, accompanied by a definite plan for its obtainment, followed by an action plan. Simply put… plan, purpose and action.

You were destined for greatness; you can have an impact on this planet. You were born to make a difference.

I challenge you to become this person! Start now! Success is not a destination; it's not a place where you arrive. Success is a direction. No matter your current condition; no matter where you are right now. Whether deep in debt or positioned at the top of a major company, you are successful if your thoughts are, and you are *marching on* to a better you. Being broke is a temporary condition and being poor is just a state of mind.

This means that you are to seek and find your Purpose, your Passion, and you're Chief Aim in Life. God has placed greatness in each and every one of us; it is your job in life to find what that greatness is and let that greatness propel you towards your destiny. The reason why I said you are to find your purpose is because your path in life has already been pre-planned for you. And if you find that path, you will live the good life which God has prearranged and made ready for you to live. You have been born with a chosen assignment.

You were not born to the race you want to run, that race has been picked already for you. You were born to discover your race and if you find it, you will also find the path to the good life. Because you have been born to fulfill the thing that God has graced and anointed you to do. Grace is a gift from God, you didn't earn it nor did you have to work for it, it was your gift. All you have to do is receive it by faith and it's yours. That means God has graced you to do your job exceedingly and exceptionally well with excellence. You must discover your path; you must discover your race. Remember, you are not here just for any reason, your life has been pre-planned, it's been purposed by God for you to fulfill a certain path.

We think it's alright to live our lives the way we want to live and keep trying to choose our race instead of discovering the race that was chosen for us. If you discover your path, your race, you will be fruitful in everything you set your hands to do.

I was no different from you. I selected my race (a professional major league baseball player) without giving one thought to finding out if that was my true race. All I wanted to do is play professional baseball as long as I could then retire with millions of dollars, but that wasn't God's plan for my life. I accomplished part of my race that I created for myself.

I was blessed to receive a college athletic baseball scholarship from the University of Nebraska – GO BIG RED! And was selected (drafted) by the Philadelphia Phillies Major League Baseball Club. I thought I was on my way to fulfilling the race I chose, then one day during the first inning of a game during my first spring training, something happened, I now call it my "**One Shining Moment**" I had a career ending injury.

With one swing of the bat, my entire life changed. During that '*at- bat*' I tore every ligament and cartilage in my knee ending my career as a major league baseball player. Because of that one moment in time, it changed my race forever. I went back to school and graduated with a computer science degree and a few years later got an advanced MBA degree from the University of Georgia as well.

I have worked for some of the largest IT companies in the U.S. and those companies have sent me around the world, paying me salaries I could never have dreamt of. My plan was not to finish college; I only went to college to play baseball, to give me the opportunity to go pro. I would have never chosen technology as my profession. But my race was already predetermined beforehand; all I did was found what God had intended for me to do. Now I'm loving life to the fullest. I have sweat-less victories, I have the grace of ease on my life and everything my hands touches proposers.

This book will prepare you to find and obtain employment, but until you know what your true purpose is, you will not, you cannot, be great at anything. At best, all you will be is average! I challenge you to find your purpose in life. I challenge you to become great in your chosen field, to become an expert. Employers are always looking for experts to help get things done. You can't be great at something if you don't like it. You can't like something without being good at it. And you can't be good at anything unless you derive some satisfaction of doing it. Your Purpose, your Passion, and your Chief Aim in Life will tell you what you were born to do. "Chase your Passion, not your Pension".

So what does this mean to all you job seekers? It means before you submit one more resume or complete one more application, you must take some time to define your purpose and your passion in life. Knowing your purpose and finding your passion will reduce your stress, helps you focus your energy, simplifies your decisions, gives meaning to your life and most importantly, gives you direction on what type of employment you should be going after.

This is the secret to success; this is the seed to greatness. I would say that 95% of all Americans never find their Purpose, Passion or Chief Aim in Life because they don't even know they should be seeking it. So they go from job to job wondering why they can't find employment that fits them. That's because they are working in jobs they hate because they are not great at it. Employers are always looking for greatness. But all we want is a pay check.

During these tough times, you cannot afford to go to work just for a pay check. If you do, you will find yourself on the unemployment line over and over again. Dare to be great! Discover your purpose and pursue it with effort. When I was pursuing what I was supposed to be doing, I just didn't sit there and it just came to me one day. No, I tried a lot of different things, that's one of the reasons why I have had so many different jobs. I was pursuing my purpose.

You will have to pursue your purpose; it's not inevitable that you will walk in it. It's not simply that something happens and you end up in your purpose, you have to pursue it with all your might. Seek and find your true calling. Find your Godly purpose, your expected end for your life and don't stop until you find it.

**Step 2: Creating your Resume**

I have chosen to write the writing your resume part towards the end of this section, to indicate to you that the format of your resume is NOT the most important part to finding employment. I will not spend a lot of time discussing this topic, because contrary to popular belief, your resume format is not that important. Also, as I mentioned before, never spend any money having someone else write your resume. You possess the skills to write it yourself.

You have skills that employers want. But those skills won't get you a job if no one knows you have them. Good resumes broadcast your abilities. They tell employers how your qualifications match their job's responsibilities. If these critical skill sets are constructed well, you have a better chance of landing interviews—and, eventually, a job. The availability of personal computers and laser printers has raised employers' expectations of the quality of resumes. E-mail and online applications help employers sort and track hundreds of resumes.

Let me address one thing before I go further. This has to do with "cover letters". Back in the day, every resume would and should have been accompanied by a cover letter.

Failure to provide one would mean your resume would probably have been deleted. That's not the case any longer. Because of technology, employers are only reviewing resumes. I personally have never and I mean never read or reviewed one cover letter when looking for a new hire. And I have personally NEVER in the past 10 years or so submitted a cover letter with my resume. It's a waste of time, so don't do it.

Technology has also given resume writers greater flexibility; page limits and formatting standards are no longer as rigid as they were several years ago. "The only rule is that there are no rules". Resumes should be error free—no typos or spelling mistakes—but beyond that, use any format that conveys your information well.

However, the no-rules rule does not mean anything goes. You still have to consider what is reasonable and appropriate for the job you want. Advertisements for a single job opening generate hundreds of responses. Busy reviewers like me, often spend as little as 15 seconds deciding whether a resume deserves consideration.

Listed below is a six step checklist for creating resumes that will help you pass the 15-second test and win interviews. I will provide you with information on how to format resumes, describe what information your resume should contain, address how to highlight your skills for the job you want, and cover the different types of resumes typically used during job searches.

**a. Your resume should be no longer than two-pages long.** The rule of thumb is, if you have 8 years or less of experience your resume should only be one-page long. If you have 9 years or more, then your resume could be two-pages long, but no more.

For example, a long resume is difficult for me to read and given the volume of resumes I receive, long resumes are often deleted. If your resume doesn't match this pattern, it probably contains unnecessary words or irrelevant information. Eliminate anything that does not help prove you're qualified for the job.

**b. Gathering and Organizing the Facts.** Start working on your resume by collecting and reviewing information about yourself: previous positions, job duties, skills, accomplishments, and education. These are the raw materials of your resume.

**c. Contact Information.** This includes your name; permanent address, phone number, and e-mail address. Place your full legal name at the top of your resume and your contact information underneath it. This information should be easy to see, reviewers who can't find your phone number can't call you for an interview. Also, make sure the outgoing message on your voicemail sounds professional. And remember to check your e-mail inbox regularly.

**d. Qualifications Summary.** The qualifications summary, which evolved from the objective statement, is an overview designed to quickly answer the employer's question "Why should I hire you?" It lists a few of your best qualifications and belongs below your contact information. A qualifications summary is optional. It can be particularly effective for applicants with extensive or varied experience because it prevents the important facts from being lost among the details.

**e. Experience.** Resumes should include your job history. The name and location of the organizations you have worked for, the number of years you've worked there, title of your job, a few of the duties you performed, and results you achieved. When describing your job duties, emphasize results instead of responsibilities and performance rather than qualities. It is not enough, for example, to claim you are organized; you must use this section to prove it.

**f. Education.** You should list all relevant training, certifications, and education on your resume. Start with the most recent and work backwards. For each school you have attended, list the school's name and location; diploma, certificate, or degree earned, along with year of completion; field of study; and honors received. If you have not yet completed one of your degrees, use the word "expected" before your graduation date. If you do not know when you will graduate, add "in progress" after the name of the unfinished degree.

**Choose a Format.**

There are three main resume formats: chronological, functional, and combination. I recommend using only chronological.

Chronological - This resume type is the most common. It organizes your experience around the jobs you have held. This format is an excellent choice for people with steady work histories or previous jobs that relate closely to their career objective. To create a chronological resume, list each position you have held, starting with the most recent and working backwards. For each position, give the title of your job, name of the organization you worked for, and the number of years you worked there. Next, relate the duties and accomplishments of that job. When describing your jobs, you should use action statements, not sentences. Instead of writing "I managed a fundraising campaign," write, "Managed a fundraising campaign." Use strong verbs to begin each statement. Be specific, but not overly detailed in describing what you did. Three to five statements are usually sufficient for each job. And no job should have more than four consecutive lines of information under it as large blocks of text are difficult to read. If you must use more space, find some way to divide the information into categories.

Your most important positions should occupy the most space on your resume. If you've had jobs that do not relate to the position you want, consider dividing your experience into two categories: Relevant experience and other experience. Describe the relevant jobs thoroughly, and briefly mention the others. If you have had many jobs, you probably do not need to mention the oldest or least important ones. Just be careful not to create damaging gaps in your work history. For a sample chronological resume, I have included my personal resume in (*Appendix H – Personal Resume*) for your review.

**Proofreading.**

Take time to prepare the best resume you can. You might not be the most qualified candidate for every job, but your resume might be better than the competition. The most common mistakes are simple typographical and spelling errors. Computer spelling checkers do not catch correctly spelled words used incorrectly—"of" for "on," for example, or "their" for "there." You want your resume to stand out, but not for the wrong reasons. Avoid mistakes by having several people proofread your resume for you. Before you send out your resume, review the vacancy announcement and *fine tune* your resume to meet the employer's criteria. Sprinkle your resume with language found in the position description, paying special attention to your qualifications summary if you have one.

Lastly, this section is for the 40 and over age group who believe that they are being discriminated against in the job market because of their age. I don't subscribe to that subscription! I'll be discussing this later in more in detail. Your resume should only show the last 10 years of work and do not put any graduation dates on your college degrees as well. Why?

**Reason #1:** At the end of the day, employers only care about "What have you done lately". The market place changes so rapidly that your job you did 5 years ago will probably have nothing to do with your current job or the job you are trying to obtain. So concentrate your resume experience on only your last 10 years.

**Reason #2:** With only the last 10 years of experience showing on your resume and no dates on your degrees, an employer won't know how old you really are. On the other hand, if you put more than 10 years of work experience and add dates to your education, as a hiring manager, I can calculate how old you are within 2 – 3 years. I have been using this approach for over 10 years and have never had one interviewer ask me about when I graduated or what was I doing in year "11". So don't worry about it.

**Step 3: Creating Your Lists**

Create a short list of companies you would like to work for that fit your skill set or qualifications by capturing each company's career job posting website URL link. For example, if you are in the healthcare field then you would select companies like McKesson, Emory University Hospital, WellPoint, and Kaiser just to name a few. Select about 15 – 20 companies. Use Google to find their websites and make your way to their career job posting section and save that link in a spreadsheet. I have included a sample template in *Appendix A*, for you to use.

Next, create a giant master list of companies. On the next page is a list of websites that will assist you in constructing your personal list. If you are not interested in driving around your metro area or traveling around the country, I suggest you limit your company selections to those companies that are in your general living area. Do not select any companies that do not have a presence in your metro area.

First go to your "Chamber of Commerce" and capture your area's top companies and save them in an excel spreadsheet. Make sure you capture their career posting website URL as well. That way when you have to go back to check for opportunities, it will save you some key strokes, which in turn, saves you time. Since most employers are seeking to avoid recruiter fees and advertising costs. These employers list all openings they have on their own company websites. So I want you to do a Google search on the following to capture your giant master list of companies:

50,000 top firms recruiting online
The Fortune 1000
The Fortune global 500
The INC 500
The NASDAQ 100
Fortune's 100 fastest growing firms
Fortune's 100 best firms to work for
Fortune's 50 top firms for minorities
The 500 largest private firms
Forbes best small firms
WSJ 100 largest public firms
WSJ 100 largest financial firms
Business Week 100 technology firms
200 Top firms for women
100 best charities
Federal Government Jobs

I have just given you the ability to access 97% of the published jobs market, somewhere around over 300,000 firms. Moreover, I just put virtually the entire published job market, millions of openings at your fingertips. A revolutionary breakthrough for any job hunter, with this process you won't need to go anywhere else to search for a job. Here you can get directly to employers of interest and see what job openings they have posted.

Why do you need both short and giant master lists? Your **short** list of companies should be no more than 20 – 30 companies. This list should be reviewed in its entirety every Monday morning to find employment opportunities. You start from the first company to the last one every Monday. Why? Because employers add opportunities every day to their job posting websites and you need to be reviewing their site weekly. Remember, these are the companies that you have a passion to work for, so give these companies your undivided attention every week.

Your **giant master** list are companies you have found by searching the internet and capturing their career section website URL's. You must make sure that you have well over 300 companies for you to traverse to find employment opportunities. This list should be traversed Tuesday – Friday each week. This will be a very large list, so make sure you select companies you know your qualifications fit very well based on the job description.

**Step 4: The Job Search**

Start with your "Short List of Companies" and begin clicking on the website URL link of the company in which you are seeking employment. This link will take you right to their career job posting section, enter your log-on information and begin looking for opportunities.

Go through your complete short list of companies and submit your resume to **only** the opportunities that fit your skill set or qualifications. What most people do is submit their resumes to every job opening they see, without giving any forethought about whether or not they qualify for the position. When you do this, your resume gets thrown out because your qualifications do not match the hiring criteria. But what it really does is waste your time and the company's time as well. Your time is wasted by submitting your resume and their time is wasted by reviewing that resume. This is the most important part, **(ONLY SUBMIT YOUR RESUME TO OPEN POSITIONS THAT YOU ARE QUALIFIED TO WORK!)** This should take only one day to peruse your short list. Do this each week without fail.

Tuesday thru Friday begin skimming through your "Giant Master List of Companies". Begin with the first company checking their career website and make sure you go thru this entire list by Friday. You must do these two searches each week without fail. You must commit to searching through your short list and giant list each week without fail.

The final step is to use one or two of the many job posting websites mentioned earlier. Spend no more than one day each week searching these websites. I suggest using **Indeed** www.Indeed.com, and **CareerBuilder** www.CareerBuilder.com. Using these two sites will give you about 90% of the open positions on the entire job posting websites. But remember, never submit your resume using their websites, find the company that posted the opportunity, go to that company's website, and submit your resume using their job posting website.

**Step 5: Creating your Profile**

Each time you find an opening at a company's website, make sure you create your own personal profile to capture your personal information, resume, user id and password. Use the template in *Appendix B* to capture all your user ids and passwords. This shortcut will save you time because every visit on a company's website will require you to identify yourself by inputting your user id and password. This effort will also prevent you from forgetting or misplacing your log on information.

**Step 6: Networking: Get the word out**

Many companies are using internal referrals. Call everyone you know. The job they interviewed for last week and didn't get might be your new job.

I'm a Baby Boomer and must admit I didn't use Social Networking to find employment. I don't use any of the popular tools which include MySpace, Facebook, "LinkedIn", Twitter, Friendster, Ning, Orkut, Bebo, KickApps, MOLI, Fast Pitch and Plaxo. The only tool I am registered on is LinkedIn, because it is a primary business network that has more than 135 million members in over 200 countries and territories. I know you have heard that companies use this social media for employment opportunities, but that's really not the case. This technology is still slightly ahead of its time. Because of our current economic situation, most companies don't have to use this type of tool to find candidates. What most companies prescribed to doing is posting open job opportunities to their career websites and wait for the resumes to come pouring in. Companies don't have to search for anyone these days. Therefore, I never waste time using this type of communication for employment. Below are three actions to use with regards to networking:

**a. Tell everyone all the time**. There is no stigma that you are looking for a job right now, so the more people who know you're looking, the more likely you'll find a job. Matter of fact, I received my last three jobs because of someone telling be about the job opening. So make sure you tell everyone.

**b. Build your network before you need it**. No matter if you are looking for employment or not, having a strong network is a good form of job security. Don't wait until times are tough to nurture your network. The key to networking is first, it's not who you know, it's who knows you. Second, great networkers are not thinking about "What can this person do for me?" To the contrary, they are thinking, "What can I do for this person?"

**c. Concentrate on LinkedIn**. If you do decide you want to use Social Networking, then I recommend that you only concentrate on LinkedIn because of the following information:

- As of September 30, 2011, LinkedIn counts executives from all 2011 Fortune 500 companies as members; its corporate hiring solutions are used by 75 of the Fortune 100 companies.

- More than 2 million companies have LinkedIn Company Pages.

- There are now more than 180,000 unique domains actively using the LinkedIn Share button on their sites to send content into the LinkedIn platform. Referrals from LinkedIn to publisher sites around the Web are up more than 75% between June 30, 2011 and September 30, 2011.

**Step7: Interviewing that will get you employed**

As I told you before, I'm a hiring manager and have been one for over 15 years. I've seen good and bad interviews, but mostly bad. The method of interviewing at my company begins with a 30 minute telephone interview. If the candidate passes this interview, we bring them in for a four hour long face-to-face interview.

It's an intense four hours and the candidate has to be ready to answer one question; "What can you do for me"? What "Value Added Proposition" (VAP) can you bring to our company to help solve a problem? This is the bottom-line question which all employers want YOU to answer. The better you can answer this question, the better chance you stand at getting hired. You must be in the problem solving business. Everything you do and say in the interview must address this VAP question.

Before I address the VAP for you, let me address something else. I am going through hiring candidates right now and I must say I have been very disappointed thus far. Not because of the candidates addressing the "Value Added Proposition" (VAP) question but rather their interviewing etiquette (dress, grooming & manners). So allow me to address this first.

**Interviewing Etiquette (Dress, Grooming & Manners):**

The best rule of thumb is to "always" dress in professional businesslike attire. Make sure you look like a million bucks. Trust me when I tell you, the interviewers will notice. Dress to impress. In most cases, that would require a suit or conservative sport coat and business slacks with tie. Shoes should always be polished and not severely worn. Men's suits should be blue, black or gray and if at all possible cleaned and pressed as well. White shirts are still preferred.

One of the side benefits of being professionally dressed is that it makes you feel more confident and at ease with a stressful situation. Skillful interviewers will often invite you to remove your coat or tie during the interview. DO NOT do it, even if you are on a tour of their site or dirty areas. Keep your professionalism on guard at all times.

Avoid heavy make-up, colognes or perfumes. You are there to get a job, not a date! Also ladies, minimize **jewelry** to prevent projecting an image that will distract from the completion of your mission. I say this because, I interviewed a young lady and she wore about ten bracelets on each arm. Every time she moved her hand or arm those bracelets made so much noise I could not hear her speak. It was so distracting I could not concentrate on our conversation. Needless to say, she did not get the job.

You want to present a clean cut, conservative image to a potential employer. Your appearance will be complemented by your manners and demeanor. Be courteous, polite and appreciative (but not subservient) with all that you meet; from the receptionist to the president. You should project a confident (but not cocky) presence to all who meet you and you can easily keep your enthusiasm maintained by simply focusing on the potential rewards of this process, a job!

Good etiquette begins before you arrive! If you are detained for whatever reason, stop and call. Most companies will have provided you the number for that purpose and the old saying applies - "If you call, you're never late." Plan to be at the location 10-13 minutes early to allow enough time to find the interviewer's office and nearest lavatory. A last minute restroom stop is always in order and a few deep breaths will help diffuse any case of "the nerves."

Finally, always address the interviewer as mister or miss, until asked to do otherwise. This denotes respect for his or her position and does not rush familiarity. Try to remember the names of the people you meet. It is appropriate to ask them for a business card, this is a good way to remember their names and titles.

**Answering the Value Added Proposition (VAP) Question**

During my interviewing of candidates, there did not exist one candidate that could give an example of their Value Added Proposition (VAP). What is a VAP, you ask? Briefly, the Value Added Proposition is what you bring to an organization that the next person doesn't. What makes you or what you have to offer unique and worthwhile. You should be able to sum up your VAP in as few sentences as possible. Your VAP is a personal version of a mission statement. In much the same way that a mission statement should be clear and concise, so should your Value Added Proposition. In effect, you are selling yourself to a company in the same way that an organization is selling itself to its customers via its mission statement.

For example, my VAP is **"I get things done...PERIOD".** Companies can count on me to do what I say and say what I do; ALWAYS. That's called ACCOUNTABILITY. As your experience changes, so will your VAP. The more projects you take on and the more time spent in your field, the better your VAP will be.

Therefore, consider your VAP to be an evolving statement of what you have to offer; a living, breathing, tag line, so to speak. And my tag line is ACCOUNTABILITY!

When you interview, employers are looking to see what you can do for them. It is the age old WIIFM factor, "What's in it for me?" Employers wants to know why they should hire you, what you are going to provide for them in terms of cost savings, reduction in time or resources, increased sales/revenue, etc. It is when you can provide an employer with the answer to a need they didn't recognize they had, that you will find yourself on the receiving end of the offer. So, I ask each and every one of you to sit down and figure out your Value Added Proposition.

**How to define your Value Added Proposition (VAP)**

Every interview I go to, I have already determined what my VAP will be for that employer. Below are **three** actions I used to create my Value Added Proposition:

***Action 1***

***Define what you are good at and what you are not***

**Get in the zone and stay there** – Find out what you do well and keep on doing it. Don't ask what I'm doing right; ask what I'm doing WELL?

a) Make it your mission to find out your strengths. Discover what you don't like doing and stop doing it". This is the fire that fuels sustained individual success. This is the discipline of getting things done! You need to work with your strengths and manage around your weaknesses. Weaknesses reveal little about strengths.

b) Knowing your strengths. The most common interviewing mistake is the inability to discuss your job strengths. Why? Because most job seekers, like yourself, do not take the time to think about all the things you do every day in the workplace. When you know how to do something, you do it automatically. So get to know your strengths.

c) To excel in your chosen field and find everlasting satisfaction in doing so, you will need to understand your unique strengths. You will need to become an expert at finding, describing, applying, practicing, and refining your strengths and talents. *This is the secret to sustained success (i.e. making the greatest possible impact over the longest period of time) lies in knowing yours strengths.*

- What will guarantee sustained success is: discover your strengths and cultivate them. Build your careers and live around them and discover what you don't like doing and stop doing it

***Example: Batting Practice in Major League Baseball***

You might think batting practice in the major league is just guys going to the plate and swinging at anything that comes their way. But that is far from the truth. If you ever go to a major league baseball practice or get to the game early enough to watch batting practice, 90% of all the activity is centered on batting practice. Why is that? Because each player needs to find and recognize their "Strength Zone", their "Sweet Spot", their "Kitchen", so with every swing; they are finding, describing, applying, practicing and refining their strength to themselves.

Once they define that zone, they tailor their swing to only go after that pitch. Therefore, batting practice is only swinging at pitches that come into their zone. Professional baseball players do this so much that they train their mind, eyes, hands and feet to only swing at the pitches in their zone. The great players do this so well, that they take their minds out of the loop and whatever their "eyes" see, their hands and feet reacts to. They do it so much and so well, it becomes automatic! The great professional major league baseball players don't think about the pitch that is coming, they only react to what their eyes see and their hands are connected to their eyes. So whatever their eyes see their hands will swing automatically if the pitch is in their zone.

How do you think a major league baseball player can decide to swing at a 90 mph pitch within less than two seconds? He can do this because he has trained his eyes and hands to only swing at his strength zone pitch.

Anytime a player recognizes a pitch that is **not** in their zone, they don't swing, they take it! This is precisely what you should do! You should know your zone pitch, your sweet spot, your strength zone (*i.e. a near perfect performance in an activity that you derive some happiness from and you can do it repeatedly*) so well that you can do it automatically without thinking. GET IN YOUR ZONE AND STAY THERE!

Unfortunately, most of us have little sense of our talents and strengths. Instead, we are guided by our parents, family, teachers and friends to go in professions that have little to do with our passion, strengths or talents. We become experts in our weaknesses and spend our lives trying to repair these flaws, while our strengths lie dormant and neglected. So what are strengths?

**What are Strengths?**

- ✓ Strengths consist of near perfect performance in an activity
- ✓ For an activity to be a strength, you must be able to do it consistently and you must derive some happiness from it
- ✓ An activity is a strength only if you can see yourself doing it repeatedly, happily and successfully

Strengths are something you can do well right now. An employer will hire you because of your strengths. These strengths tell the employer if you have the necessary background and experiences to do a good job. Everyone has strengths. What are yours?

Knowing your job strengths also allows you to plan a more effective job search. You will have greater success by picking job openings that match what you have done before and what you already know how to do. If there are not a lot of jobs using your strengths, then you might want to consider getting retrained in something that the marketplace has a demand for. Try to match what an employer is looking for with the strengths you have learned from other jobs.

By thinking about your strengths in advance, you will choose jobs better suited for you. You'll be more confident in interviews, you'll know how to write better resumes and you'll find a job that is more satisfying.

I highly recommend you read a book by Marcus Buckingham entitled "Standout." This book is a revolutionary new book that has an online strength assessment tool which will unveil your top two strength roles and offers sharp, practical ideas that everyone can use to find their edge and win at work. This book contains a unique identification number that allows you access to his website at http://www.standout.tmbc.com. Once you know which two strength roles you have, you can leverage them for powerful results for personal and career development.

I have included in *Appendix E (Personal Unique Strengths),* my personal VAP unique strengths list for your reference. As I said before, my VAP is "**getting things done through LEADERSHIP**"! I've learned good leadership always makes a difference. I have seen what good leadership can do. I personally witnessed Louis Gerstner at IBM turn around an organization that was on the brink of closing its doors for good.

He positively impacted the lives of thousands of individuals. Everything lives or dies by way of leadership, and I have made it my business to become the best leader I can be for an organization. That's my VAP.

***Action 2***

***Creating your 30 second (Value Added Proposition VAP)***

**Your VAP Elevator Pitch** - An elevator pitch is a short summary used to quickly and simply define your value added proposition. The name "elevator pitch" reflects the idea that it should be possible to deliver the summary in the time span of an elevator ride, or approximately sixty to ninety seconds or less.

The problem is **too few people are prepared to deal with such a situation**. They haven't considered what they would say, much less prepared something to say or previously rehearsed. As a result, instead of capitalizing on the opportunity, they just let it walk out the door. But not you; listed below are action steps to help in these types of situation.

At some point in the interviewing process, every job seeker will be confronted with a question along the lines of, "So tell me about yourself?" How you answer this question will make or break you.

a. Your VAP pitch must be concise, direct and to the point. You want to make it clear to prospective employers that you are a team player and will get along well with others.

b. Your VAP pitch must be compelling. You need to make sure that your interviewer(s) understands that you possess some knowledge or skill that will help them solve the problems they are facing.

c. Your VAP pitch must be conceptual. During your elevator pitch; you don't want to get into the specific, daily duties of the jobs you have held. Instead, you should just talk about your skills and the projects you have completed at a high level.

d. Your VAP pitch is NOT a rehash of your resume. Employers want to hear about your real-life attributes and skills.

I have included in *Appendix F (Personal VAP Elevator Pitch),* my personal VAP elevator pitch for your reference. I have used this pitch or some variation of it for over 15 years and it has served me well. I challenge you to create your own VAP elevator pitch and memorize it so when you are asked the question, "So tell me about yourself?" You will have an appropriate answer that addresses WHY YOU!

***Action 3***

***During the Interview***

**Memorizing your VAP pitch and unique strengths** – by completely memorizing your VAP pitch and strengths you will display the confidence and attitude that most employers are looking for. If your pitch and strengths match what the employer is looking for, you will get an offer.

Once you have ascertained the company's needs, you must continuously answer the question "*What can you do for me*?" This is best accomplished by giving examples of accomplishments you have previously achieved for companies that are relevant to the position for which you are interviewing. **The basic theme of any interviewing process is that behavior tends to repeat itself.** Winners continue to be winners and losers are continuous losers.

Past behavior is the best predictor of future behavior. Whatever the interviewer finds a pattern of the past they will assume it will repeat in the future. Like it or not, your past accomplishments are the manifestations of your present worth. Remember that the interviewer's interest in you is purely selfish. It is no different than your selfish interest in the company. They want to hire the person who can do the most for them. **All attention should be focused on what the company wants and your agenda should**

***temporarily*** **take a backseat**. If the focus of attention is on you, you will get into trouble or find yourself in trouble.

**During the interview, you should concentrate on only two things:**

- Making the interviewers like you and respect what you could do for them

- Gathering as much information as possible

If the hiring manager(s) believe that you will accomplish their objectives, you will be considered for employment. Being liked helps get you an offer.

Information gathering helps you assess the interview when you get back home. Trying to process information during the interview causes mistakes! Don't do it. You will have plenty of time after the interview to decide if this is a good career move. Keep your focus on the objective of the interview, which is getting an offer of employment. **The best strategy is to try your best to be in a position to get an offer**. You can always decline it.

You must know and be prepared to discuss why you want to change employers, including reasonably detailed explanations for each past job change and your accomplishments for every employer, ideally expressed in dollar values. Interview processes are usually characterized by suspicion on all sides. Both sides fear mistakes. Not giving specific enough information about your career, accomplishments and motivating factors usually lead to negative inferences on the interviewers' part.

## The Importance of First Impressions

While it's nice to think that the world is a place of measured judgments, where everyone is given equally complete consideration, that's not how the real world works.

***The problem is that everybody's busy***

People have too many things to do and too little time to get it all done. As a result, instead of giving people the time and consideration that people think they deserve, people are much more likely to rely on gut instincts and make up their minds quickly because that gives them more time to spend on everything else. That means when employers make a basic evaluation of a candidate for hire, they often make up their minds in 30 seconds and in some cases as little as 6 seconds. That includes me!

I'm in the process of hiring two program managers and the first thing I notice is how the candidates are dressed. I notice everything; if their shoes are shined or not, if their suit or dress fits well or not; if their hair is well groomed. **I notice everything!** My old college baseball coach used to say "You only play as good as you look"! Remember this saying: "**How you look speaks so loud I can't hear what you say…**" The first impression is the only impression. If you want to be able to survive and thrive in this world, you have to deal with it as it is. That means dealing with the fact that people often take remarkably little time to make very important decisions. So make sure you always look the part.

**Answering interviewing questions**

Again, the interviewer doesn't want to hear a recitation of your resume. By the time he's interviewing you, he's already read your resume, and he knows you're qualified. That's not an issue, anymore. You wouldn't be in their office, if it were. They now want to hear about your real-life attributes, your real-life skills. But they won't tell you what those are; they are waiting to hear it from you.

Remember what I said: ***"The person who gets the job is not the most qualified for the job; it's the person who is the most qualified at getting a job"***. If you don't remember anything else, remember that quote! This includes preparing in advance to answer every question an interviewer might ask. You may wonder, "How is it possible to know in advance what an interviewer might ask?" There are only a few questions that an interviewer will ask, remember, they are looking for someone they can count on. I have already given you 50% of the answer, by having you create and memorize your VAP "Value Added Proposition". Every answer to every question should be addressed around your VAP.

Every interviewer is ready to hear what you can do for them. So when the interviewer asks the question: "Tell me about yourself", your answer should go right into your VAP, which describes your strengths and how they will help the interviewer and the company get things done.

It's very important to practice your responses to normal interview questions. For this purpose, I've listed some sample questions that you should become proficient in handling before your interview. The use of a tape recorder and a practice partner will make this preparation easier and more effective. Be prepared for at least one very open ended or surprise question right at the start such as:

- Why are you interested in working for our company?
- Tell me about yourself - who are you, really?
- What can you do for us?
- Why should we hire you?
- Why are you leaving your current company?
- What things are important to your job satisfaction?
- What accomplishments in your current job are you most proud of?
- What are your most difficult (or most rewarding) job responsibilities now?
- What particular strengths and weaknesses do you have?
- What do you know about our company?
- What are your short and long term career goals & how do you plan to reach them?
- How would your associates describe your personality?

- How do your spouse and children feel about this career move?
- Which of your past jobs did you like the least (or the best)?
- What did you like (or dislike) about your last supervisor?
- What kind of people do you find most difficult to work with?
- How has your current job prepared you to take on more responsibility?
- Tell me about one of your biggest mistakes and how you handled it?
- How would you rate yourself on a scale of 1 to 10 in terms of ambition?
- What are you looking for in the next job?
- What aspects of your job do you consider most crucial?
- How did you choose your college? How did you pay for it?
- Do you prefer working with others or alone?
- Describe the work environment in which you felt most comfortable?

- Have you ever resigned or been fired from a job? Why?
- How well do you take direction or coaching?
- How long have you been thinking of changing jobs?
- Can you work under pressure?
- Describe a situation where your work was criticized. How did that make you feel?
- Why have you changed jobs so frequently?
- Why have you been out of work so long?
- If you could start over, what would you do differently in your career?
- What do your subordinates (supervisors, peers) think of you?

**Salary Requirements Question**

Never leave the "expected compensation" area blank" when filling out a job application. Fill in the required salary amount you want for that job. If it's too high, they will tell you and that's when the negotiation begins. You should always complete the "current compensation" questions with your total current compensation package spelled out (including base salary, bonuses, commissions and overtime). Fielding questions on salary requirements is particularly difficult for many candidates. The odds are said to be 6,000 to 1 of your guessing the exact figure that a potential employer has in mind while talking with you. So don't try and guess.

For example, when I'm asked for my salary requirements, I don't stumble or stutter; I look them right in the eyes and give them a number. Not a range, but ONE number. Because I know my value and what I bring to their organization, and I also know what the marketplace for my position is paying. So when an interviewer asks you the question: "What's your salary requirement?" You give them one number. You give the interviewer one number, which should be at least $10,000 above your current (or last) salary level. Normally, anything over a 15% salary increase will be considered too high, unless you are working from a low base or are looking at a major career move.

To find out what the marketplace is paying for your position of interest, visit:
http://www.salary.com/mysalary.asp.

**Questions you should ask**

There comes a point in the interview, where you are asked, if you have any questions. The answer to that question should always be YES I do! I can't tell you how many times I have asked that question to a candidate, just to hear "no I do not." At this point, a very shrewd thing to do is to pull out your questions list from your portfolio or binder, and start from question number #1.

You need to have your questions prepared in advance, these questions are important. The questions you ask, including the words you select to express them, will strongly influence the interviewer's assessment of you. These questions prevent you from overlooking needed information. After the interview, you can easily determine the information you still need to get and this information will help you decide whether this opportunity is right for you. Preparing the lists of questions will make you much more organized and efficient. **The interviewers will notice**. I always did! Moreover, the answer to your questions will prepare you for your closing statement. Having questions for the interviewer is strongly advised.

This will make it crystal clear to the interviewer that you took the interview seriously and were prepared. Pay close attention to the answers that the interviewer gives you when you ask him question number #1 from your list. (*What kind of person are you looking for to fill this position? And what is your ideal job candidate like?)* The interviewer is getting ready to tell you exactly what they are looking for.

You need to capture this information by writing it down next to question number #1 and let the interviewer see you write it down. This will be the beginning of your closing statement. Go through every question on your list one at a time! Pay close attention to every answer given; capture each answer by writing it down next to the question. I have included my personal interviewing questions for your reference in *Appendix G (Interviewing Questions).*

**The Interview Close and Follow-Up**

It will be obvious when the interview is drawing to a close. Only three things can happen at this stage:

1. You'll be asked back for a second interview

2. You'll receive an offer

3. You'll be rejected based on this interview

Obviously, you want to leave every interview with either the first or second outcome. You'll recall that your objective in any interview is to solicit an offer that would make you want to accept the position. Put another way, you can't accept or reject an offer that is never made!

**If by the end of your interview you are interested in the position, ask for the job.** I can't tell you how many times I had a solid candidate to hire and he/she walked right out of the door without asking me for the job. This is one of the reasons why I'm so successful at obtaining employment, because I ALWAYS ask for the job. And if the candidate would have just asked me, I would have hired them on the spot. This is part of your VAP!

When asking for the job, this shows that you have the fortitude and confidence to ask for what you want. "You have not, because you ask not". So ask for it, you will be amazed of the reaction for the interviewer when you ask for the job. Be ready, because they just might make you an offer right on the spot.

This does not commit you to anything. It will positively affect compensation. It may be the difference between getting an offer or a rejection letter. Tell the key interviewer (probably also your supervisor-to-be) that you are interested in working not only for the company but for them personally. Interviewers like to hear positive things too. If the "chemistry" is good between you, they need to know it so they'll go to bat for you.

Close with these words, **"I am very interested in what I have learned here today and the opportunities that this position presents. I believe I would enjoy working here and learning from YOU as well. Is there anything more you need to know about my background to ensure we go to the next step of the process, because I WANT THIS JOB!!!!**

Then give them your "**PERSONAL GUARANTEE".** You look them right in their eyes and say, "Mr./Ms. interviewer, if you select me, I give you my personal guarantee and I promise you won't be sorry or disappointed in hiring me". Then shut up and wait until they speak.

If you are not interested in the job, DO NOT USE THIS STRATEGY! You see, employers are ALWAYS looking for someone they can count on. It's called accountability. That means the employer can count on you to get the job done, no matter what. And when it comes down to it, that's what every hiring manager is looking for in his/her staff. That includes me as well. It is perfectly OK to ask when you can expect to hear from the employer, but you should not mention other opportunities for which you are being considered. Close with a firm handshake and a sincere "thank you" to the interviewer for their time.

Good taste dictates that you should e-mail a follow-up note within 24 hours! It should be short and direct; it should be addressed to the main interviewer or the person to whom you'll report. The email should again thank them for their time and consideration and ask for the job! It should portray you as being confident and ready to meet the challenges of the position. By mentioning the others with whom you talked, it will be obvious that you were attentive, interested in the needs of the employer and anxious to be a member of their team.

The timing of this e-mail arrival is critical since one of its purposes is to distinguish you from other interviewees the company may have seen in the interim. Another objective of the email is to demonstrate your writing ability. It also presents an excellent opportunity to recap your problem solving abilities and make specific mention of major projects or tasks that the company wants to address in this hire. Having said all this, it is good to remember that common sense is the most important thing you can bring to any interview. Interviews are, after all, a purposeful exchange between two parties with common interests. There is no substitute for good preparation and a conscious effort in preparing for good interviews. However, your ability to "think on your feet" may well separate you from the crowd.

You may not succeed on every interview but you'll clearly improve your odds of success with every good attempt you make! As Vince Lombardi once said, "practice does not make perfect, perfect practice makes perfect."

It is critical that you have the correct spelling of the names of the people you have met, their titles and addresses. If a second interview is the next likely step, be sure also to get the names and titles of those who you'll see on that interview. The closing is an excellent time to probe the interviewer with questions about how they see your strengths and shortcomings. It is also timely to reinforce your abilities. Do not show disappointment if you don't receive encouragement at this stage. It can very well be one final test of your ability to deal gracefully with rejection.

**Final Thoughts on Interviewing**

**Never lie or be dishonest**. Many catastrophic things can occur if you do this, especially if you get the job. **Overstating and/or stretching the truth is lying**.

Do not get drawn into even a low-key argument; if a statement you have made is challenged, quietly stick to your position. If possible, hedge with statements like "In the environment I have been in, this is how it was handled. If there are better ways to do it, I would be very interested in learning them." Even if the interviewer disagrees, you are exhibiting a willingness to be reasonable and flexible. Remember, the interviewer may be testing you by playing the devil's advocate. If you argue, you cannot win even if you are right.

I have given you everything you need to be an outstanding interviewer. I've showed you the following:

1. What your appearance should be when you walk through the door

2. How to find your strengths and how to develop your Value Added Proposition (VAP), including your Elevator Pitch

3. How to address interviewing questions

4. Why you should have your own questions to ask the interviewer

5. How to close and "ask" for the job

Most people equate job interviewing as very difficult. Anxiety is a normal reaction but it can be minimized by knowing what to expect. A frequent mistake interviewees make is to appear too casual OR too anxious. Find a friend or family member to help you practice interviewing. Use "Employmentology" to guide your answers. Now you are ready to have your first interview. If you are not successful the first few times, don't worry, just keep interviewing. Sooner or later, if you don't give up, give in, or quit; someone will offer you a job! **I promise you!!!**

Lastly, you might be tempted to tell a hiring manage, that you can do anything and you can learn anything. What that just told me, as a hiring manager is, "You can't do anything and you don't know anything". I am not in the business of training someone from scratch. I'm looking for someone who can hit the ground running with little to no training or supervision. Therefore, I recommend you not saying the above. You must show them what you can bring to their organization that will solve a problem. I said this before and I'll say it again: "You must be in the problem solving business".

Chapter Six

# OUR CHANGING ECONOMY

*If it's to be, it's up to me!*

This section has a lot of statistical analysis. I'm a numbers guy and numbers give you a better picture of the truth.

**US Economy: Overview**

The US has the largest and most technologically powerful economy in the world. In this market oriented economy, private individuals and business firms make most of the decisions. Federal and state governments buy needed goods and services predominantly in the private marketplace.

At the same time, US firms face higher barriers to enter their rivals' home markets than foreign firms face entering US markets. US firms are at or near the forefront in technological advances, especially in computers and in medical, aerospace, and military equipment; their advantage has narrowed since the end of World War II.

The onrush of technology largely explains the gradual development of a "two-tier labor market" in which those at the bottom lack the education and the professional/technical skills of those at the top and, more and more, fail to get comparable pay raises, health insurance coverage, and other benefits. Since 1975, practically all the gains in household income have gone to the top 20% of households, which is every family making over $80,000/Yr.

The global economic downturn, the sub-prime mortgage crisis, investment bank failures, falling home prices, and tight credit pushed the United States into a recession by mid-2008, making this the deepest and longest downturn since the Great Depression.

In 1993 I came across an economics expert named Harry S. Dent, Jr. And over the past 18 years, I have read all his books which are listed below. The data source of this chapter is taken from these books.

1. The Great Boom Ahead
2. The Roaring 2000
3. The Next Great Bubble Boom
4. The Great Depression Ahead
5. The Great Crash Ahead

Mr. Dent created a term called "Spending Wave" which predicts the health of our economy by moving forward the birth index 47.5 years. Why this number? That's the average age at which consumers like you and I reach our predictable peak in spending. By our mid-forties, the average American family has purchased the largest home we'll own and all the furnishings to go with it, and we spend money on clothing, food and education for our teenage children. Once the children leave the nest, the fixed costs remain the same but variable costs suddenly start dropping. Thereby marking the end of the necessary family spending that drives the economy.

***The essence of the Spending Wave is simple: Predictable spending patterns drive the economy.***

People represent about 70% of the Gross Domestic Product (GDP) and represent the largest influence on our economic health. As larger groups of consumers age and spend more, the economy grows. When large groups in the population pass their peak stage in spending, the economy slows down. And this is exactly what is happening right now in our economy.

## The Baby Boom Generation

I'm from the Baby Boom Generation (Boomers). The Boomer Generation, 92 million American children were born between 1945 and 1964. In America, boomers are widely associated with privilege; we grew up in a time of affluence. As a group, we were the healthiest and wealthiest generation of all time, and amongst the first to grow up genuinely expecting the world to improve with time. The Boomers control over 80% of personal financial assets and more than 50% of discretionary spending power.

We are responsible for more than half of all consumer spending, we buy 77% of all prescription drugs, 61% of OTC (over the counter) medication and 80% of all leisure travel.

It is important to focus on the size of this generation, because the size of this generation gives it power. It's the number of people all doing the same thing at the same time, creating a "Thundering Herd". The Boomers have changed every part of the economy as we passed thru and we have left something behind. EXCESS CAPASCITY! The reason is because the generation behind us (Gen X) is a little bit smaller. This is why no political program is going to generate strong growth in the next decade or raise job creation.

The boomers will no longer have an ever growing appetite for consumption. Things have changed. The boomers are focused on saving and paying down debt as we age. We have taken our credit cards and went home! By in large the boomers are saving for retirement to live comfortably. What does this means to you? It means that our economy is not and will not get any better from what you see right now! At least not for the next 10 years or so! Our current unemployment rate now is hovering around the 8% range.

**The Subject of Retirement**

While I have your attention Baby Boomers, let me address the subject about **RETIREMENT**. Stop thinking and talking about retiring. We are not like our parents, we are not tired or worn out, and our jobs have not broken us down to the point where we need to rest our mind and body. As a group, we are the healthiest and wealthiest generation to date, and we are amongst the first to grow up genuinely expecting the world to improve with time. We are a special generation, very different from those that had come before us.

Our generation, the Baby Boomers, have been described variously as a "shockwave". Because of the sheer force of our numbers, we are a demographic bulge which remodeled society as we passed through it. That includes **retiring**! This notion of retiring at the young age of 65 is ludicrous. Stop thinking about retiring and continue working.

**History of Retirement**

Retirement began in the United States, when large numbers of aging factory workers were slowing down assembly lines, taking too many personal days and usurping the places of younger, more productive men with families to support. A number of older employees were causing great unemployment among younger workers by refusing to retire. Retirement was a necessary adaptation, but the old employees were not going quietly.

By 1935, it became evident that the only way to get aging employees to stop working for pay was to pay them enough to stop working. A Californian, Francis Townsend, initiated a popular movement by proposing mandatory retirement at age 60. In exchange, the Government would pay pensions of up to $200 a month, an amount equivalent at the time to a full salary for a middle-income worker. Horrified at the prospect of Townsend's radical generosity, President Franklin D. Roosevelt proposed the Social Security Act of 1935, which paid retired workers age 65 and older, and disabled people, a fixed amount each month for life.

In 1935, the program was funded by a 1% tax on both employers and employees on the first $3,000 of a worker's earnings. In January 2006, nearly 34 million Americans collected Social Security, with the average retired worker receives approximately $1,000 per month. Today, the Social Security tax rate is 7.65% on employers and employees. The United States of America can NOT sustain this government entitlement program. Because there are more of us (Baby Boomers) than there are of the next generation (Gen X), with our sheer numbers we will bankrupt the system as we know it. The reason it's working now, is because again of our large numbers, there are more of us working today than there are older people retiring.

This is why we should continue to work until the end of the world or until we die. This is only possible if we find ourselves producing work which is our labor of love. That's why it is so important to find and cultivate your purpose, your passion, and your chief aim in life. You cannot work in a profession for 30 – 40 years if you don't love what you are doing. If you continue to work, you will not have to worry about whether there is enough in Social Security or do you have enough in your 401(k). Our economy would take a boost as well, because we would continue to spend, maybe not like we were spending in our 40's, but nevertheless, we would continue to spend.

**Economics 101**

Please stay with me here; I'm going to have to give you a short course in ***"Macroeconomics"***. You need to understand why our economy is struggling to get back to its glory years of the 1990's, and why it's so difficult finding and obtaining employment. Macroeconomics deals with the performance, structure, behavior, and decision making of our entire economy. Meaning everything is connected.

As I mentioned before, many years ago I came across a book called "*The Wealth of Nations*" by Adam Smith. This book was published in 1776, the year of America's Declaration of Independence. This book is over 1200 pages in length, it took me months to finish reading it. I am NOT suggesting that you read this book, unless you have a keen curiosity for macroeconomics. After reading this book, I began to understand how our free market economy really works.

As mentioned above, the United States of America is a "**Market-Driven**" economy. It's a system for exchanging money for goods and services. This system enables buyers and sellers to come together and engage in transactions. In a *market economy*, consumers and businesses decide what they want to produce and purchase in the marketplace, ***with little government intervention***. They make this decision by voting with their dollars.

**Remember this**: "*Producers decide what to produce given the demand they see in the marketplace in terms of their sales and the price they get for their goods and services.*" I'll come back to this later. Our economy is not a true market driven economy, but a mix between market and command. Where both market forces and government decisions determine which goods and services are produced and how they are distributed.

Macroeconomic output is measured by Gross Domestic Product (GDP). GDP is the sum of all spending on goods and services in our nation's economy. Consumption by consumers (you and I), investment by businesses (buying & selling of products/services; including employing you and I), and government spending are the three major parts of our economy. It also includes foreign trade by exporters and importers, which is a net zero or, oftentimes, a bit on the negative side. Spending by consumers (you and I), which is called "***consumption***", is by far the largest part of the U.S. GDP. It accounts for an average of about two-thirds of GDP.

*The composition of GDP breaks down roughly as follows:*

| | |
|---|---|
| Consumption | 70% |
| Investment | 15% |
| Government | 20% |
| Net Exports | -5% |
| | 100% |

I'm highlighting this for you because each component of GDP is important. Before I'm done, I will show you why. **Stay with me, I will connect all the dots to show you why you need to know this so you can be better prepared at finding the "Job of yours Dreams"!**

After reading *The Wealth of Nations* I read its counterpart; "*The General Theory of Employment, Interest, and Money*" by John Maynard Keynes. This book is over 380 pages in length. Again I would NOT suggest you read this book either, unless you have a passion for economics. The premise to *Keynesian Economics* is: The prescription for a sluggish economy is to use government spending to prime the pump. *Keynesian economics* is an approach to economic policy that favors using the federal government's power to spend, tax, and borrow to keep the economy stable and growing. ***Does this sound familiar?*** This is the economic policy that our government is following right now. This is NOT the policy that the United States should be following. Because our federal government is using what is called **Quantitative Easing (QE).**

QE is an unconventional monetary policy used by our federal government to stimulate the national economy when conventional monetary policy has become ineffective. A central bank buys financial assets to inject a predetermined quantity of money into the economy. This is distinguished from the more usual policy of buying or selling government bonds to keep market interest rates at a specified target value. QE has been nicknamed "printing money". With QE, the term printing money implies that the newly minted money is used to directly finance government deficits or pay off government debt.

Here is why this won't work, remember the "Spending Wave"? This wave predicts the health of our economy by predicting the spending peaks. The Baby Boomers are done with paying for the largest homes as well as for all the furnishings to go with it, and we are done with spending a lot of money on clothing, food and education for our teenage children.

This is the end of *Keynesian Economics.* This comes back to the basic argument, a twenty-five year trend in Baby Boom spending, from 1983 – 2007, this trend has peaked and our economic growth will slowly run into at least the year of 2020 and perhaps until as late as 2023. This declining wave of spending is not something you can fight with a few trillion dollars in stimulus here and there. And our U.S. Government has already spent more than anyone thought they would spend.

We are headed for a rise in interest rates that is about to hit the United States, probably somewhere in late 2012 or first part of 2013. It would take tens of trillion of dollars to off-set this natural down-ward trend that we are currently in and a necessary shift to saving an aging generation that is the deepest in debt of any generation in our history. More importantly for the near term, the greatest debt and credit bubble in history peaked in 2008 at $56 trillion dollars! The United States faces a total debt of at least $102 trillion dollars, which is 7-times GDP. In contrast, our total debt only reached two times GDP during the roaring 20's boom.

What the U.S. Government should do is NOT use stimulus to try and revive our economy that is already very much wounded and needs to be deleveraged and rebalanced. However, the U.S. Government should use the debt to help cover the losses that banks incur from actually ridding down loans to their real values. Such a move would have the potential to save well more than $1trillion dollars per year in interest and principal payments by consumers and businesses for years and decades to come. This solution is a real stimulus plan that is focused on the root cause of this economic crisis.

An out of control debt bubble and the aging of the massive Baby Boomer Generation, has led to a decrease in consumer spending and that trend is only going to increase after 2012 when the Baby Boomers really hit their slowing stage after age 50.

My fellow Americans, we have choices; we can choose to bury our head in the sand and ignore the changing world around us all the while hoping for the best, but doing nothing.

Or we can choose to recognize that the time we just left, that time of growth and seemingly easy prosperity that marked most of the past three decades are over for now. What lies ahead will be difficult, but through education and proactive efforts we can not only see what lies ahead but we can also profit from it. As you might expect, this section is helping you in choosing that education and prosperity. Our economy is going to experience a deeper down turn and deflation in prices; not inflation. This comes predicatively once in a life time about once every 80 years. Which means that very few people will understand what is happening. The largest generation in history will be spending less and saving more for retirement, which are trends that follow aging.

The ratios of those unemployed to find jobs are roughly 5 to 1. Meaning for every one open position there are 5 people for that one job. This means the competition for the unemployed is fierce. With over 100,000 new workers coming into the economy every month and very little increase in hiring the situation only becomes worse over time. Over the next several years we are likely to see unemployment get even higher and remain high with the worse unemployment rates occurring sometime in 2013.

This means employers have the upper hand in not only who they hire but what they pay as well.

Therefore, we will suffer business, bank and job losses unlike anything we have dealt with in our lifetime. Crashes of this magnitude will not happen again for another 60 years or more. I am here to wake you up to the greatest financial crisis of our life time! I want to shake you up so you can save yourself, your family and your business from financial ruins before it's too late. So what does this mean to you as an American and a job seeker?

The Baby Boom Generation is not spending because their kids are leaving the nest and they as consumers are more interested in saving for the next stage of their lives, RETIREMENT! This trend of kids leaving the nest will accelerate from 2012 forward making the demographic down trend more obvious and the government's efforts to fight it more difficult. Businesses having recognized that the Baby Boomers spending patterns has changed have lowered their output to match the level of demand. **This is the root cause of "unemployment"!**

**Connecting the dots**

I hope by now you understand why our economy will not rebound to the glory years, no matter what our federal government does. I will now attempt to connect the dots for you. Our economy is driven by consumer consumption and the more we buy stuff the better off our economy. The Baby Boom Generation, 92 million strong, is the largest in

US history and now we are beyond our peck spending years, therefore, we have stop spending and began to start saving for retirement. The next generation behind us, Gen X is a smaller generation and they are NOT at their peak spending years yet and won't be for at least 10 – 15 years. **And that's causing our economic down turn and our unemployment.** So no matter how much more money the government throws at our economy in terms of stimulus packages, it will not be enough and it will NOT work.

Remember: *Producers decide what to produce given the demand they see in the marketplace.* So let me address this right now. The Baby Boomers are no longer spending; producers are no longer producing as much because of the lack of demand for their products and services. Companies only hire more people when demand for their products and/or services increase, thereby, increasing the company's revenue stream. ***I repeat again, companies only hire people when they have an increase in demand for their products and services… PERIOD!*** Our federal government CANNOT CREATE JOBS!!!! No matter what you hear from Washington, being from the Democrats, Republicans, Tea Party or anyone else. Let me be crystal clear; WASHINGTON CANNOT CREATE JOBS! And if they do create federal government jobs, those jobs are paid for by our income taxes which increase our federal debt.

Companies do not hire because they receive tax incentives from the government. What the government has done with giving tax incentives is letting them keep more money in their pockets and paying less to the tax base of America. Just because companies have more money in their pockets will not make them go out and start hiring people. Remember, the only factor that allows companies to hire people is the increase of demand for their products and services. So whenever you hear anyone from Washington saying they are going to create more jobs, know this, they are not telling you the truth. So now you know.

### Final Thoughts on the Economy and Employment

In this difficult economy, steady employment becomes even more important than it is in normal times. So if you are employed stay there! You need to become an expert at your job. You need to find ways to make yourself indispensable to your employer. So first thing tomorrow morning go into your manager's office and ask three questions.

**Question 1**: What can I do to make the greatest amount of impact over the longest period of time for you and this company?

**Question 2**: What are the biggest challenges that you are facing in this department?

**Question 3**: What are the most important problems that I can solve that will make your job easier?

Your employer has hired you to do one of the following things: save them money, make them money, or be more efficient by saving them time. You must be in the problem solving business! Once you find out the answers to the above questions, begin working on solving these problems. You need to develop your primary differentiator. Your differentiator is the single most important thing that sets you apart from anyone else.

Employers are looking for greatness. Become great at what you do. You need to schedule weekly meetings with your manager to go over the status of these three questions. Your employer is looking for "Accountability", someone they can trust to get the job done. And if you do this, you will not have to worry about being unemployed and if you find yourself unemployed, you won't be for very long.

On a personal note, our government (Washington) was not established to create jobs for individuals. Washington was established to run the United States of America. It's our responsibility as a citizen of this great country to obtain the necessary education and work experiences to show enough added value for a company to want to hire us. It is your responsibility not the government to find and obtain employment. So stop looking for Washington to bail you out, you've got to go out and find the job of your dreams. Your mantra should be: ***"IF IT'S TO BE, IT'S UP TO ME"!***

Chapter Seven

# GENERATION Y

*The Unemployed Generation – But not YOU!*

Generation Y (age 25 and under), also known as the Millennial Generation, Generation Next, Net Generation, **Echo Boomers**, and Worst Generation describes the demographic cohort following Generation X. There are no precise dates for when the Millennial generation starts and ends, and commentators have used birth dates ranging somewhere from the mid-1970s to the early 2000s. Members of this generation are children of Baby Boomers. Some say that this generation is just as large or larger that the Baby Boomers. These are the young adults who are 16 - 25 years and younger.

With the youth unemployment rate in the U.S. reaching a record level at 17%, it has been argued that this unemployment rate and poor economic situation has given

Generation Y a new name called "**The Unemployed Generation**". These economic difficulties have led to dramatic increases in youth poverty, unemployment, and the numbers of young people living with their parents. Between 2005 and 2011, the proportion of these young adults living in their parents' home increased, according to the U.S. Census Bureau. The percentage of men age 25 to 34 living in the home of their parents rose from 14% in 2005 to 19% in 2011 and from 8% to 10% during this period for women.

**Education, Employment & Earnings**

Everything begins and ends for you, (Echo Boomers) with education. In September 2011, the Census Bureau released a study called "*Education and Synthetic Work-Life Earnings.*" It examined the economic value of educational attainment by estimating the amount of money that people might earn over the course of a 40-year career given their level of education. They showed that a person with bachelor's degree working full time from ages 25 to 65 would have $1 million dollars more in earnings than a similar person with just high school diploma.

The level of education has risen steadily in America over the last 70 years. In the 1940 Census, 24.5% of people aged 25 and over had at least a high school diploma. In 2008, 85% of this group had at least a high school diploma, and 27.7% had a bachelor's degree or higher. In addition, 10.2% of people aged 25 and over had advanced degrees.

Occupation is often the mechanism by which education is related to earnings. Higher levels of education allow people access to more specialized jobs that are often associated with high pay. Degrees in many occupations are treated as job training that may be required for a position or earn the employee more pay within that position. While this report does not focus on the specific occupations individuals hold, it does consider the degree of labor force involvement.

In addition to higher earnings, people with higher levels of education are more likely to be employed full-time, year-round, that is, they held a job for the entire year and worked in a full-time capacity. In fact, 68% of people with a doctorate are employed full-time, year-round compared with 38% of people with less than a high school diploma. At every level of education, people working less than full-time; year-round have earnings that are lower than those who have full-time, year-round employment. This information helps us to better understand the interaction between education, employment, and earnings—higher earnings are both the result of higher likelihood of full time employment and the higher level of education required for that employment. I'm telling you all this because if you want to get and stay employed for now and for the future you must obtain a higher level of education than just a high school diploma.

There is a myth out here in the marketplace, which says it's hard to get employed because I'm a boomer; over 40 years old. **That is NOT true!** Statistics shows that the boomers have significantly increased its labor force participation rate and is projected to exhibit further increases in the future. A number of factors are responsible for the increase in the participation rates of older workers since the late 1980s. First, the boomers are living longer and have a healthier lifestyle, so older people are working more years to earn additional income. In addition, the high cost of health insurance has forced many older workers to remain in the labor force in order to keep their employer based health insurance or to return to work in order to obtain health insurance through their employer.

In addition, changes in Social Security laws since 2000 have raised the normal retirement age for certain birth dates and decreased the benefits for early retirement. The modified laws were intended to discourage workers from early retirement and encourage increased participation of older workers in the labor market. These changes also established credits for delayed retirements, and that has encouraged older workers to delay their retirement and benefit from higher income for each additional year of work. It is not the Baby Boomer Generation that is having a hard time finding employment, its Generation Y **(Echo Boomers)**. Here are the reasons:

**Let me tell you what I see.** I see a whole new generation of students going to college and taking the wrong majors and receiving the wrong type of degrees. Not only are these young people going after the wrong degrees they are graduating with an average of around

$50,000 in student loan debt. This is totally unacceptable! Because these college grads are not getting the right type of degrees, their salaries are not at the level to sustain paying off their loans; consequently, these students are defaulting on their student loans at a record pace. But this will not happen to you! Let me say this, it does not matter which school you attend as long as it's accredited. Harvard, Yale, University of Michigan, Stanford or even Wayne State University (my alma mater), they are all the same. In today's marketplace, experience is the name of the game.

As a hiring manager, I would hire a college student with the right type of degree(s) and at least two-years of actual work experience in their chosen field of study that attended a lower-level university versus a student that went to one of those high priced, top level universities with no actual work experience. Therefore, find a school that you can afford. **Your goal is to graduate with the least amount of student debt as possible.**

I was blessed to receive an athletic scholarship and a few government grants that paid for my undergraduate degree; therefore I had NO loans when I graduated. I was heads and shoulders ahead of my friends who were inundated with student loans that they had to pay back. So if you have to go to a community college for a couple for years to keep your cost down, then do so. Do whatever it takes to make sure you do not become burdened with long-term debt obligations associated with student loans.

If you want to be successful for now and for the future, you must get in an industry that is expanding and growing. Industries and occupations related to health care, personal care and social assistance, as well as construction are projected to have the fastest job growth between 2010 and 2020, according to reports by the U.S. Bureau of Labor Statistics. Total employment is projected to grow by 14.3 percent over the decade, resulting in 20.5 million new jobs. Despite rapid projected growth, construction is not expected to regain all of the jobs lost during the 2007-09 recession.

The following is a list of the top three industries for the future:

- ❑ ***Health Care***
- ❑ ***Educational Services***
- ❑ ***Food Services and Drinking Places***

**Health Care**

- Recognized as the fastest growing and the largest industry; healthcare will provided 14.3 million jobs for wage and salary workers.
- Ten of the 20 fastest growing occupations are healthcare related.

- Healthcare will generate 3.2 million new wage and salary jobs between 2011 and 2018, more than any other industry, largely in response to rapid growth in the elderly population.

- About 40 percent were in hospitals; another 21 percent were in nursing and residential care facilities; and 16 percent were in offices of physicians.

- The healthcare industry consists of the following segments

  - Hospitals
  - Nursing and residential care facilities
  - Offices of physicians
  - Offices of dentists
  - Home healthcare services
  - Offices of other health practitioners
  - Ambulatory healthcare services

**Outlook**

Many job openings should emerge in all healthcare employment settings as a result of employment growth and the need to replace workers who retire or leave their jobs for other reasons.

Wage and salary employment in the healthcare industry is projected to increase 22% through 2018, compared with 11% for all industries combined. Employment growth is expected to account for about 22% of all wage and salary jobs added to the economy over the 2011-18 periods. Projected rates of employment growth for the various segments of the industry range from 10% in hospitals, the largest and slowest growing industry segment, to 46% in the much smaller home healthcare services.

Employment in healthcare will continue to grow due to many contributing factors. The proportion of the population in older age groups will grow faster than the total population between 2011 and 2018. In addition, older persons have a higher incidence of injury and illness and often take longer to heal. As a result, demand for healthcare will increase, especially in employment settings specializing in gerontology care for the elderly. Employment in home healthcare and nursing and residential care should increase rapidly as life expectancies rise, and families are less able to care for their elder family members and rely more on long-term care facilities. Many of the occupations projected to grow the fastest in the economy are concentrated in the healthcare industry. For example, over the 2011-18 periods, total employment of home health aides is projected to increase by 50%, medical assistants by 34%, physical therapist assistants by 33% and physician assistants by 39%.

Also demand for dental care will rise due to greater retention of natural teeth by middle-aged and older persons, greater awareness of the importance of dental care, and an increased ability to pay for services. Dentists will use support personnel such as dental hygienists and assistants to help meet their increased workloads. Tougher immigration rules that are slowing the numbers of foreign healthcare workers entering the United States should make it easier to get a job in this industry.

**Educational Services**

- Educational services are the second largest industry, accounting for about 13.5 million jobs.

- Most teaching positions, which constitute nearly half of all educational services jobs, require at least a bachelor's degree, and some require a master's or doctoral degree.

- Retirements in a number of education professions will create many job openings.

Workers in the educational services industry take part in all aspects of education, from teaching and counseling students to driving school buses and serving cafeteria lunches. Although 67% of workers in educational services are employed in professional and related occupations, the industry also employs many administrative support, managerial, service, and other workers. Teachers account for 47% of all workers in the industry.

**Outlook**

Greater numbers of children and adults enrolled in all types of schools will generate employment growth in this industry. A large number of retirements will add additional job openings and create good job prospects for many of those seeking work in the field of education.

Wage and salary employment growth of 12% is expected in the educational services industry over the 2008-18 periods, comparable to the 11% increase projected for all industries combined. Over the long-term, the overall demand for workers in educational services will increase as a result of a growing emphasis on improving education and making it available not only to more children and young adults, but also to those currently employed and in need of improving their skills.

Much of the demand for educational services is driven by growth in the population of students at each level. Low enrollment growth projections at the secondary school level are likely to limit growth somewhat, resulting in average growth for these teachers. However, enrollment growth is expected to be larger at the elementary (grades 1-5) and middle school (grades 6-8) levels, which will likely result in slightly higher employment growth for teachers at these levels. Reforms, such as universal preschool and all-day kindergarten, will require more preschool and kindergarten teachers.

Due to continue emphasis on the inclusion of disabled students in general education classrooms and an effort to reach students with problems at younger ages, special education teachers will experience relatively strong growth. School reforms calling for more individual attention to students will require additional teacher assistants, particularly to work with special education and English-as-a-second-language (ESOL) students. Enrollments are expected to grow at a faster rate in postsecondary institutions as more high school graduates attend college and as more working adults return to school to enhance or update their skills. As a result, postsecondary education will experience a faster growth in the industry as a whole. In addition to job openings due to employment growth, retirements will create large numbers of job openings as a greater-than-average number of workers are over the age of 55 in nearly all the major occupations that make up the industry—from janitors to education administrators.

**Food Services and Drinking Places**

- Food services and drinking places provide many young people with their first jobs; about 1 in 5 workers in this industry were 16 to 19 years old, about 5 times the proportion for all industries.

- Nearly 3 in 5 workers in this industry worked as cooks, waiters and waitresses, and combined food-preparation and serving workers.

- About 2 out of 5 employees work part time, more than twice the proportion for all industries.

- Job opportunities will be plentiful because large numbers of young and part-time workers will leave their jobs in the industry, creating substantial replacement needs.

Food services and drinking places may be the world's most widespread and familiar industry. These establishments include all types of restaurants, from fast-food eateries to formal dining establishments. They also include cafeterias, caterers, bars, and food service contractors that operate the food services at places such as schools, sports arenas, and hospitals.

Wage and salary jobs in food services and drinking places are expected to increase by 8% over the 2008–18 periods, slightly less than that 11% growth rate projected for all industries combined. Numerous job opportunities will be available for people with limited job skills, first-time job seekers, senior citizens, and those seeking part-time or alternative work schedules.

A growing population that increasingly prefers the convenience of eating out and having their meals prepared for them will contribute to job growth and a wider variety of employment settings in which to work. All sectors of the industry are expected to generate numerous jobs. The number of limited-service eateries and fast-casual restaurants that specialize in serving soups, salads, and sandwiches made to order on the spot will grow as time-strapped diners seek out healthful menu alternatives while on the go. In contrast, traditional fast-food and quick-service restaurants that appeal to younger diners and those consumers whose first priority is convenience should increase more slowly than in the past.

Job opportunities in food services and drinking places should be very good, because the large number of young and part-time workers in the industry will generate substantial replacement needs. A large number of job openings will be created for new entrants as experienced workers find jobs in other, higher paying establishments, seek full-time opportunities outside the industry, or stop working. The greatest number of job openings will be waiters, waitresses, combined food preparation and serving workers all which also have high replacement needs.

Graduates of college hospitality programs, particularly those with good computer skills, should have especially good opportunities at higher end full service establishments. The growing dominance of chain affiliated food services and drinking places also should enhance opportunities for advancement from food-service manager positions into general manager and corporate administrative jobs.

Now that you know where the jobs will be in the future, you should make sure you prepare yourself for those types of positions. Below are the steps you should take to make sure you are not one of those people who can't find employment.

**6 Steps to Gainful Employment**

1. **Seek And Find Your Purpose, Passion, Chief Aim In Life**. You cannot truly be great at anything until you absolutely know what you were born to do. Greatness is already in you, it came with you when you were first born. It is your job to seek and find what moves you, what you love to do. Find it! And once you find it, it will propel you to your destiny.

2. **Discover What Your Strengths Are**. Make it your mission to find your strengths. This is the fire that fuels sustained individual success. This is the discipline of getting things done! To excel in your chosen field and find everlasting satisfaction in doing so, you will need to understand your unique strengths.

3. **Education Is Where it All Begins & Ends**. You will need to have more than a high school diploma. Statistics indicates that the unemployment rates for persons between the ages of 16 to 24 are higher if you do not have at least a 4-year college degree. People with a bachelor's degree had lower rates of unemployment than those with less education in every month from January 2008 to December 2011. This period included all but one month of the recent recession, which began in December 2007 and ended in June 2010. This is an important milestone in our history according to the Census Bureau. For many people, education is a sure path to a prosperous life.

The more education people have the more likely they are to have a job and earn more money, particularly for individuals who hold a bachelor's degree. If you dropped out of college, go back and finish your degree. If you have never enrolled in college before, then enroll. You need to differentiate yourself from everyone else. Just having a high school diploma alone won't cut it anymore. In this country, 85% of people have at least a high school diploma, and 30% have a bachelor's degree or higher. In addition, 11% of people aged 25 and over have advanced degrees. You will not be able to compete without an advanced formal education.

4. **Get The Right Degree**. Back in my day, it didn't make a difference what type of college degree you got, as long as you got one you were just fine. Companies would hire you just because you had a college degree, mainly because not many people had college degrees back then. That was their differentiator, what set them apart from anyone else. But now it seems like everyone has a college degree and your strategy must now be laser-focused on a particular field or industry. You cannot afford to get a general studies degree (e.g. business administration, criminal justice, psychology, philosophy, or any other general knowledge degree). You must get a degree that has a particular job or career associated with it. For example, if you receive a

computer science degree, that degree prepares you to become a computer programmer. Likewise, an engineering degree prepares you to be an engineer. If you get a general business degree, that degree does not prepare you for a particular job.

5. **Get Co-Op & Intern Experiences**. Don't you dare go to college and just settle for a degree without work experience. Let me tell you what will happen if you don't follow this step. You will obtain your degree and find yourself working at the "FootLocker" selling sneakers or working at a bank as a teller. Because that's the only thing that your degree without work experience will prepare you for. If it takes you another 2 or 3 more years to graduate, then so be it. Employers hire people because of their work experiences. Remember, employers are only concerned with addressing one question and that is: What can you do for me? (i.e. can you save me money, can you make me money, or can you be more efficient by saving me time). Employers are hiring you for a reason; you must connect your work experience with one of those reasons. This is your differentiator!!! This will set you apart from all of your colleagues who have decided not to Co-Op or Intern.

6. **Select The Correct Industries**. You need to connect your degree(s) to a growing and expanding industry. Above, I have given you the top three industries for

now and the future. These are large industries, you must research them. The "*Occupational Outlook Handbook*" by U.S. Bureau of Labor Statistics" is an excellent reference book. It contains which jobs will be available in these industries and a lot more. This information is in *Appendix I* for your review.

In summary, this Generation (Gen Y), the unemployed generation is currently experiencing difficulty finding and obtaining employment. You have two generations ahead of you, the Generation X and the Baby Boomers that are still in the work force. And neither generation is ready to retire right now. So you have to do more and be more to stand out during your job search.

The Baby Boom generation will move entirely into the 55-years-and-older age group by 2020, increasing the age group's share of the labor force from 19.5 percent in 2010 to 25.2 percent in 2020. The "prime-age" working group (ages 25 to 54) is projected to drop to 63.7 percent of the 2020 labor force. The 16 to 24-year-old age group is projected to account for 11.2 percent of the labor force in 2020. I'm telling you all this for a reason. You must start now to be prepared for the workforce of tomorrow.

Over the next ten years, 54.8 million total job openings are expected. While growth will lead to many openings, more than half, 61.6 percent will come from the need to replace older workers who retire or otherwise permanently leave an occupation. In 4 out of 5 of the fastest growing occupations, openings due to replacement needs will exceed the number due to growth. Replacement needs are expected in every occupation, even in those that are declining. More than two-thirds of all job openings are expected to be in occupations that typically do not need postsecondary education for entry.

I've given you an abundance of information in this chapter from a hiring manager's prospective. If you follow these instructions you will get hired. I guarantee it!

Chapter Eight

# LET'S TALK ABOUT MONEY

*One of the secrets to becoming wealthy is you MUST first decide to be*

I am so confident that if your follow my instructions in the book, you will get employed. I would like to spend a little time discussing the subject of MONEY. Brace yourself my friends because the time has come for some very plain talk about you and your future. You have come a very long way on the road to employment so far, and you have reached a gate through which you shall have to pass. It is titled "*Let's Talk About Money*". After you pass through this gate you will know how to make the most of your money. Because you will not always be unemployed! That is a fact.

Men and women have been concerned about money since the first coin was fashioned in Asia Minor about 700

B.C. You might say that money is like good health, in that we are concerned about it to the extent that we don't have it. The purpose of this chapter is to get down to the basics, to clear the air surrounding the entire subject of money. To do this, I'm going to get absolutely elementary. While you may already know most of the things I'm going to write about; I think it's important that I remind you exactly what money is, how much of it enough is, and how to earn the amount of money you need to live the way you want.

To begin, let's dispel the old myth, once and for all, that money is bad or unimportant. It is not bad, and it is important. It is just as important as the food and clothes it buys, the shelter it affords, the education it provides, and the doctor's bills it pays. Money is important to any person living in a civilized society. Nothing will take the place of money. That's all there is to it. What is money? Money is the harvest of our production. Money is what we receive for our production and service. We can then use it to obtain the production and services of others. We can, quite often, accurately gauge the extent of our production and service by simply counting the amount of money we received for it.

Try to remember this formula: ***The amount of money you receive will always be in the direct ratio to the demand for what you do, to your ability to do it, and to the difficulty of replacing you.***

In our economy, a highly skilled and educated person is worth more money than a person who is not highly skilled and educated and can be easily replaced. This is not to say that one person is any better or more important than any other person. Remember that, in this writing, I'm writing about only money -- nothing else. To nine-tenths of the world's population, the average American is already rich. There's a greater difference between the standard of living of most of the world's population and our average worker. There's also a difference between the standard enjoyed by an average worker and the richest person in our society.

If you want to be wealthy, there are two distinct steps you must take. **First**, you must decide exactly how much money you really want. Once this decision is made, the **second** step is to forget the money and to concentrate on improving what you now do, until you have grown to the size that will fit and naturally earn the income you seek. **I just gave you one of the secrets to becoming wealthy.** Once you're fully qualified for the amount of money you decided to earn, you'll soon find yourself earning it. You will also discover that with your new powers and abilities, it's not more difficult, perhaps even less difficult than what you are now doing for the money you are earning.

***There are really three amounts of money you <u>need</u> to decide upon:***

**1.** The yearly income you want to earn now and in the near future.

2. The amount of money you want to have in a savings or investment accounts.

3. The amount of money you want as retirement income, whether or not you ever retire from active work.

Now, it's here that most people make very serious mistakes. They never decide on any of the three amounts of money. If you will decide on these three amounts, you will automatically have placed yourself in the top 5% of all Americans. You will have a plan for your future, a blueprint for future financial accomplishments. You will know where you are going, and if you are serious about it, you will most certainly get there.

You see my friends, the trouble with most people is not that they can't achieve their goals; they can do that, all right. **The trouble is that they don't set goals!** They leave their future to chance and find out, sooner or later to their sorrow, that chance doesn't work; that they've missed the boat. It's estimated that only 5% of people decide on the money they'll earn. Thus, they take their lives, their fortunes and their futures into their own hands. You can do the same thing and you can do it starting right now! Where money is concerned, there are two kinds of people; those in the majority who cut back on their wants to fit their incomes; and those free spirits in the minority who make their incomes fit their wants. Now, which is better for you?

Let me share my story when I decided how much money I wanted to earn. I was in the workforce for about 4 years and I came across a little book titled "Think and Grow Rich", more about this book later. The book shared with me the secret to earning more income; which is, "you have to decide that you want it". I started thinking about making $100k every day. At the time, I was only making $40k a year, and then overnight I decided that I wanted to make $100k. I told my wife and she began to laugh and I did as well. And every time we wanted a good laugh I would mention that I made $100k.

Then she asked the most profound thing. She asked, "How are you going to make $100k a year, when you can't even say it without laughing?" I thought for a second and said "You are right"! So I immediately ran upstairs to my bedroom shut the door looked in the mirror. I began to say to aloud, "I make a $100 thousand dollars a year". I still laughed, at first. Eventually, the laugh turned into a chuckle, the chuckle turn into a giggle, then the giggle turned into a smile and then that smile turned into nothing.

For the first time since I said I wanted to make $100k a year, I was able to say it without any emotions. Then I put a plan together. Within 18 months of that decision, I did it! I left my current job making $40k and was offered a position with IBM, with a starting salary of $55k. During my tenure at IBM, I was promoted twice; I went from $55k to $85k then to $110K, all within 18 months. That was over 15 years ago; I've been making over $100k a year ever since. All you need is a plan, a road map and the courage to press on to your destination. Keep in mind you will have some problems and setbacks along the way. But there is nothing on earth that can stand in the way of your plan if it's backed with persistence and determination.

With the income you decide to earn written down on paper, spend a part of each day thinking of ways in which you can increase your service, the income will take care of itself. Since the amount of money you want to earn is more than you're receiving now, your part of the bargain is to find ways of increasing your service until the gap has been bridged. Have faith in God and yourself, and the quiet firm inner knowledge that you can and will accomplish your goals. Know the answers you seek will come to you in their own time, if only you keep looking for them. Above all, realize that money cannot be sought directly. Money like happiness is an effect. It's the result of a cause, and the cause is valuable service. Keep money in its proper place. It's a servant and nothing more!

Lastly, right now you may have no idea how the additional income you seek is going to come to you, or how you're going to save the amount you want in a savings or your retirement account. That isn't important. Remember, the only most important thing is that you know what you want. If you do, you will become -- you *must* become **WHAT YOU THINK ABOUT!!!** Always remain true to yourself, constantly identifying and reconsidering what is important to you and what motivates you the most. The bottom line is, "This is the greatest opportunity we as individuals have had in all of history, to design our own lives, our work, and our personal living environment to meet our own needs and dreams." Only the people who understand the logic of our new economy will achieve self-designed lives. You can do it!

Chapter Nine

# THE ROAD LESS TRAVELED

*We Become What We Think About*

I must remind you that success as a human being in modern society does not come naturally. It requires the conscious utilization of ourselves in the service of others. We have our minds, our genetic possibilities, a certain amount of time and our free will. We belong to the world minority that lives in a free society. We become whatever we seriously make our mind to become. That's possible because whatever we seriously decide to do is naturally linked to our genetic possibilities. A person with little or no aptitude for science will never decide to become a scientist. Each of us wants to succeed during this holiday on earth, and each of us should. But we don't succeed in groups; we succeed or fail as individuals.

This chapter I call *"The Road Less Traveled"*, and it contains the best basic information and the greatest ideas we need to reach whatever goal we seriously choose. I found there are very few people on this road. This road brings you success, wealth, and anything you want. **This road begins and ends within your mind!** Now let me guide you on The Road Less Traveled.

Environment is the reflection of the people who live there, change the people through education for example and the environment will change to reflect that difference. I want you to consider your own environment from your earliest memories right up to the present time. By environment, I mean the houses you lived in as a child, your neighborhood, your family itself. What was the educational background of your parents, your neighbors; and how about your environment today? Would you say your environment reflects lower, middle, or high income people? And ask yourself if the environment in which you live in now is the environment you find to be satisfactory for the rest of your life.

Putting this as simple as possible, you are where you think you ought to be. Your work is the work you think you should be doing, your car is the car you think you should be driving. Everything you do and everything you are is the reflection of your thoughts. Your world is a mirror of your thoughts! **YOU ARE WHAT YOU THINK ABOUT!!!** This I found, by far, is the greatest and strangest secret for succeeding in the world today.

Fifteen years ago I began looking for the so-called secret to success that successful people had and that unsuccessful people did not have. Not finding any successful people around me, I started buying and reading every book on success, spiritual as well as non-spiritual. In those wonderful books, I learned the importance of having faith in God, the importance of honesty, accountability, integrity, trustworthiness and believing in what's right and what's wrong. I would also add that you must be willing to fight for it. Books are filled with ideas and ideas push us into action. It was in a book that I finally found the secret to the success I was seeking for all those years.

Just as a gold miner will find things to let him know he is looking in the right places; everything I had read up to the moment of discovery, had in a way prepared me for the truth I was about to see. And one day poking about in a book store, I picked up a little book called "Think and Grow Rich" by Napoleon Hill. The title made sense to me; if one was to grow rich certainly it would come about as a result of thinking. I purchased the book, took it home and dove right into it.

Three days later I came across the secret; it was spelled out and needed no further description or definition. I read the words **"WE BECOME WHAT WE THINK ABOUT!"** That small book was the one I started looking for fifteen years before. That was the book that held the secret to success, **"WE BECOME WHAT WE THINK ABOUT,"** just six words! There are more than 600,000 words in the English language, but those were the words I needed to see, and in that order. It was at that moment that

I received the answer that I needed. It went like this: "I can determine what I think about; therefore, I can determine what I can become." In simple terms: Whatever you consciously think about is picked up by your subconscious mind and that thought is transformed into its physical equivalent by any means necessary.

Everything fell into place, people who think about wealth become wealthy and people who thinks about failing, become failures. The universal key to success is this: **As a Man Thinketh, So Is He. As You Think, So Shall You Become.** So you have the secret. You become what you think about. Now, here's the best part of all. You have in your mind everything you need to become whatever you set your mind to become.

All you need to concern yourself with is this: "Where do you go from here?" Or maybe two questions: What do you want to do and how do you get there? So get a pad and pen and begin to write everything you want to be and have. You are, at this moment the sum total of all your thoughts to this point. Simply put, you will be the sum total of your thoughts five years from now. How do you feel about that? Does it feel good, does it fill you with a warm-fuzzy feeling? If so, then you have been doing just fine and have only to continue the process. If you're not happy with yourself at this stage, perhaps it's time for a change in your thinking.

Therefore, always think of the things you want, not of the things you don't want. Your subconscious mind never sleeps; it's always working even when you are asleep. Therefore, plant in your subconscious mind any plan, thought, or purpose which you desire to translate into its physical or monetary equivalent. You cannot entirely control your subconscious mind, but you can voluntarily hand it over to any plan, desire, or purpose which you wish transformed into a concrete form.

You are in possession of the ***Master Key*** that unlocks the door to success. The master key is intangible, but it is powerful! It is the privilege of creating, *in your own mind*, a burning desire for a definite purpose. There is no penalty for the use of the key, but there is a price you must pay if you do not use it. The price is failure. There is a reward of stupendous proportions if you put the key to use. It is the satisfaction that comes to all who conquer self and force life to pay whatever is asked.

If only we would have the wisdom and patience to intelligently and effectively explore the work in which we are now engaged in. We'll usually find the success we seek, whether it be financial or intangible or both. No matter what your goal may be, perhaps the road to it can be found in the very thing you're now doing. Your mind is your richest resource. Let it thoroughly explore the possibilities lurking in what you're presently doing before turning to something new. I say that because there were probably good reasons for you having chosen your present work. If there wasn't, and if you are unhappy in the field you're in, then and only then, is it time for some serious exploration.

Now you know the secret to the "Road Less Traveled"! Stay on the road. Don't ever make a detour off of this road. This is the only road you can take to acquire all the success you seek. In closing this chapter, I will say, if you do all these things and just believe in the power of: "You Become What You Think About", then I'll see you and yes, I do mean YOU, on **The Road Less Traveled!**

Chapter Ten

# THE PURSUIT OF HAPPINESS

*It's your duty as an American to invoke the rights to become as rich, wealthy and happy as you want.*

Because you were born here in America or have become a legalized US Citizen, it is your duty to become as wealthy and prosperous as you can. That's right-- your duty! America is an empire of wealth, an empire of economic success and of the ideas and practices that fostered that success. Our economy is not only the largest in the world; it's the most dynamic and innovative as well. Virtually every major development in technology in the twentieth century originated in the US or was principally industrialized and turned into consumer products here. The ultimate power of the United States lies not in its military strength, but in its wealth, the wide distribution of that wealth among its population, its capacity to create still even more wealth, and its seemingly bottomless imagination in developing new ways to use that wealth productively.

America's wealth generating engine was created in the late 1700's by one of our Founding Father, Alexander Hamilton. He was a genius in economics, and was a scholar of human nature and knew there was no more powerful motivator in the human universe than self-interest (more about this later). He helped to create our financial system which would both channel the individual pursuit of self-interest into developing America's current economy and protect the economy from the recklessness which unrestrained self-interest always leads to. As our first Secretary of the Treasury, Hamilton was the primary author of our economic policies which we still use today. For example, the funding of the state debts by the federal government, the establishment of a national bank, a system of tariffs, and trade relationships with other countries. He put all this in place for you.

It is your God given right and your duty to become as wealthy as you can; America needs you to become wealthy. You may find that to be a very materialistic statement and perhaps, even un-American. But I beg to differ, for you to become wealthy, you will have to create a process for obtaining that wealth. There are only four ways to become wealthy: (1) inheritance, (2) winning the lottery, (3) becoming a highly paid corporate executive, and (4) creating a business that sells products and/or services to the masses. Those are the only four **legal** ways to become wealthy. The first two are by chance and the last two is how most American's have become wealthy.

You live in the most affluent county in the world, this county was created to build and acquire wealth and it starts with its citizens—YOU! One of the ways of making your millions is by becoming a highly paid corporate executive or a wealthy entrepreneur. It's your responsibility as an American to become wealthy and to promote your own self-interest. Why? Because by pursuing your own self-interest you frequently promote that of the society more effectually than when you really intended to promote it. Adam Smith, the author of *"The Wealth of Nations"* calls this action the **Invisible Hand**. For example, if you build a multi-million dollar business you will have to increase the demand for labor, which will increase your price for your goods or services; further, because the new producers also will become consumers, local businesses must hire more people to provide the things they want to consume. As this process continues, the labor prices eventually rise to the point where there is low unemployment. By becoming wealthy, you will be led by an invisible hand to promote the society's best interest automatically.

When our Founding Fathers' signed the "The Declaration of Independence" in 1776, led by Thomas Jefferson and 11 years later created "The Constitution of the United States", this gave you the right to pursue happiness in any form including the creation of wealth. I would have to safely say, that probably around 90% of all Americans have never read The Declaration of

Independence and/or "The Constitution of the United States". **The Declaration states:**

*"When in the course of human events, it becomes necessary for one people to dissolve the political bands which have connected them with another, and to assume among the powers of the earth, the separate and equal station to which the Laws of Nature and of Nature's God entitle them, a decent respect to the opinions of mankind requires that they should declare the causes which impel them to the separation. We hold these truths to be self-evident, that all men are created equal, that they are endowed by their Creator with certain* ***Unalienable Rights*** *that among these are* ***Life, Liberty and the Pursuit of Happiness****."*

That's some beautiful language. We don't use language like that anymore, that's the Kings Language. Let me break this down for you so you can understand what this Declaration has bestowed upon you as citizens of the United States of America.

Because of the war between America and Great Britain, this war plunged the British government deep into debt, and Britain enacted a series of measures to increase tax revenue from the colonies. Britain believed these tax increases were a legitimate means of having the colonies pay their fair share of the costs to keep the colonies in the British Empire. Our Founding Fathers, however, developed a different conception of the empire. Because they were not directly represented in Parliament, our Founding Fathers argued that Parliament had no right to levy taxes upon them. Therefore, they created The Declaration of Independence, which declared the causes which impel them to the separation. It also gave them the "*right of revolution*": that is, people have certain rights, and when a government violates these rights, the people have the right to "alter or abolish" that government.

The second part of the Declaration involves you and me. It states that we have certain **UNALIENABLE RIGHTS**, which means it's a right which cannot be sold and/or given away, it is yours forever. Among these unalienable rights is the right you possess to pursue happiness. This means having the right to pursue any lawful business or vocation, in any manner not inconsistent with the equal rights of others, which may increase your wealth/prosperity or develop your faculties, so as to give you your *highest* enjoyment possible. Life, Liberty and the Pursuit of Happiness means you are to live a course of living that produces extreme pleasure for yourself. Liberty means, free from restraint, you have the freedom of action that goes beyond all ordinary bounds. And lastly, pursuit of happiness means, you have the right to pursue your dream no matter how big it is, without any hindrances. This is your privilege as citizens of the United States of America.

**Connecting the Dots**

Because you are a citizen of these United States of America, you have bestowed unto you by your Founding Fathers Unalienable Rights that can never be taken away; and they are Live, Liberty and the Pursuit of Happiness. Therefore it's your duty as an American to invoke these rights at all cost. It is your God given right to become as rich, wealthy and happy as you want. Our Founding Fathers defeated Britain and created The Declaration of Independence for you! I want you to understand that the United States of America needs you to be prosperous. So get about the business of becoming a multi-millionaire promoting your own self-interest, as long as it's legal and not hindering others. By becoming a millionaire, you will have to generate a demand for your goods and services that compel others to deliver those goods and services in the most efficient manner so that you and others will be able to receive compensation from others and make a profit in doing so, which is great for our society, like an invisible hand.

When I read The *Declaration of Independence* and *The Constitution of the United States* those two documents changed by viewpoint forever. I suggest you read both of them at (http://www.archives.gov/exhibits/charters/declaration.html) while you're at it, read the *Bill of Rights* as well. I understand I have a role, a part to play in keeping America the land of the free and the home of the brave. It is our job to keep America on top by keeping our economy strong and vibrant. We do this by keeping our economy moving.

Consumer consumption keeps our economy moving; therefore America needs you to become wealthy by creating products and services for the masses to purchase which creates employment, which gives consumers more money to purchase more products and services, which requires you have to hire more people, which makes the tax base go up to fund our government, which makes the unemployment rate go down. The more you are able to do this, the stronger our economy gets the better off it is for all Americans.

I challenge you to dream big, to dream of being on the Forbes Riches People in the World list. By the way, 11 out of the top 20 on the 2012 Forbes Riches People list are Americans. And all of the 11 are self-made billionaires, creating their own fortunes from scratch. And if they can do it, you can too. So now you know, it is said that people perish from a lack of knowledge. You were born in the right place at the right time. It is your job, your duty from this day forward to pursue your dreams, to go after what's deep in your heart. Visions that can change the world might be trapped inside of you; don't be afraid to let it out. Your dreams won't make sense to everyone, so keep them to yourself. You must have courage if you are going to persevere.

So don't be afraid to face the world against all odds. Keep your dreams alive and don't let them die. If there is something deep inside of you that keeps inspiring you to try… Don't stop! Never give up; don't ever give up on yourself. Every victory comes in time that will change tomorrow. It gets easier; who's to say you can't fly? Every step you take gets you closer to your destination.

Sometimes life can place a stumbling block in your way, but you've got to keep your faith to bring what's deep inside of your heart to the light. You hold all the pieces to complete the puzzle, answers that can solve all mysteries are within you. The key that unlocks your understanding is already inside of you and you have everything you need. So keep the dream alive and don't let it die. DON'T GIVE UP!

Chapter Eleven

# CONCLUSION

*Whatever you want in life, you will have to TAKE IT and sometimes, take it by force!*

Congratulations, you made it through! Good Job! We're living in the greatest time in all of human history. There are more opportunities and possibilities available to you today than ever before. If you commit yourself to dreaming big, to becoming better at what you do, and never giving up, there is virtuously nothing in this world you cannot accomplish.

Your success in life will be largely determined by your ability to find your true calling. You must work to find the right work for you to do, and you must put your whole heart, mind, and body into doing it in an excellent fashion. You must begin to walk in the spirit of excellence. You were put here on the earth for a reason, it is up to you to seek and find that reason (your true calling). You will only truly be happy when you discover what you were meant to do. You were placed on this earth with unique skills that makes you different from all other human beings. The odds against there ever being someone just like you are more than 50 billion to one. In the entire world, there can never be someone just like you! So it's up to you to find and fulfill your true calling, because if you don't -- then you have failed. You see my friend, nobody will ever fulfill your destiny; it is yours and yours alone. If you don't fulfill it, then the world will never receive that accomplishment. Who knows, you could be the next Bill Gates.

Remember, you were placed on this earth to do something wonderful with your life. You have within you, talents and abilities so vast that you could never use them all if you lived to be a thousand years old. You have the natural skills and talents that can enable you to overcome any obstacle and achieve any goal you could ever set for yourself. There are no limits on what you can be, have, or do if you can find your true calling.

Then you will become one of the few people who are doing what they love to do. Someone who is totally absorbed in doing something that you really care about and something that is important to you. You will make more progress in a couple of years than the average wage slave makes in five or ten years.

You will come to the attention of people who can help you and open doors for you. You will be happy and fulfilled in both your work and your personal relationships. You will have more energy, enthusiasm, and creativity.

You will have higher self-esteem, and you will feel like a winner. You will unlock your true potential, and your future will become unlimited.

We live in a capitalistic society, which means, only the strong survive and the fittest live on. You were destined for greatness. You can make an impact on this planet. You were born to make a difference. I challenge you to become this person! Start now! Success is not a destination, it's not a place where you arrive, success is a journey. No matter what your current condition is, no matter where you are right now.

Being unemployed is just a temporary condition and being broke because of it is just a state of mind.

Remember, wealth is not an accumulation of things. No matter what your current possessions are, no matter what you own at this moment, if your mind is filled with wealthy thoughts and you are moving in a wealthy direction, then you are truly wealthy, NOW! Keep moving in the right direction my friend and success and wealth will be yours.

***So let me leave you with these final thoughts. First***, there is one thing I have recognized in this life and that is, life does NOT give you anything. Whatever you want in life, you will have to TAKE IT and sometimes, take it by force! The way you take it, is developing a plan and stepping through that plan until you obtain your objective. You don't always get in life what you want; you get in life what you expect. It's called "***The Pygmalion Effect***", which refers to the phenomenon in which the greater the expectation is placed upon us, the better we perform. The Pygmalion Effect is a form of self-fulfilling prophecy, if you expect the best, then that's what you'll get. You get what you expect in life not what you want in life. **I just gave you another seed to success!!!!**

***Second***, "Personal Development", which includes activities that improve awareness and identity, develop talents and potential, build human capital and facilitates employability, enhance quality of life and contribute to the realization of dreams and aspirations. When you graduate from high school or college, you go through "Commencement" ceremonies which signify the beginning, the start of something and the initiation of something new. Often times, most people think of commencement as the end.

You need to continue to grow, to read, to study, to become all you can be. ***It is said that a person who does not read is no better that a person who cannot read.*** You are the same person today that you will be tomorrow, except for the books your read, the CD's/DVD's that you listen/watch and the people you talk to. So I ask you what books have you read lately? What CD's/DVD's have you been listening and watching? And, who have you been talking to? Remember, if you are not reading, listening/watching the right things or talking with the right people, then wherever you are in life and/or whatever you have right now, that's all you will ever have or be.

So let me make a recommendation, you should spend at least 1% of your total gross income to improving your personal development. **<u>This is another seed to success</u>**; this is the path to greatness. I dare you to be GREAT! I dare you! I have included in (*Appendix I)* for your review my personal short list of books for you to read. Consider this fact: 58% of the US adult population never reads another book after high school. You should read at least two personal development books per month.

Finding a job is not easy, you must have a process; a step-by-step methodical way of finding employment. This is a recipe book! Just like any other recipe book you must follow the instructions as given. If you omit or leave out any of these instructions, then just like baking a cake you will not get the expected results. In this book I have given you the recipe to find and obtain employment. Now you have everything you need to never again be afraid of getting fired, laid-off, down-sized, or riffed. If you use this practical systematic methodology of finding employment, I guarantee you will always find your next job faster and quicker than your counter-parts. Now, go get it!!!

*************************************************

To contact Darnell Clarke, or to be placed on a mailing list to receive updates, click the "Contact" tab on his website at: http://www.darnellclarke.com. Moreover, for your convenience, all his appendix templates can be found on his website under the Templates tab as well.

## *Appendix A -Employers Short List Template*

| COMPANY | WEB | Dates/Comments |
|---|---|---|
| | | |
| | | |
| | | |
| | | |
| | | |
| | | |
| | | |
| | | |
| | | |
| | | |
| | | |
| | | |
| | | |
| | | |
| | | |
| | | |
| | | |
| | | |
| | | |
| | | |
| | | |
| | | |
| | | |
| | | |

# *Appendix B - User ID & Password List Template*

| Company | User ID | Password | Date |
|---|---|---|---|
| | | | |
| | | | |
| | | | |
| | | | |
| | | | |
| | | | |
| | | | |
| | | | |
| | | | |
| | | | |
| | | | |
| | | | |
| | | | |
| | | | |
| | | | |
| | | | |
| | | | |
| | | | |

## *Appendix C - Interviewing List*

1. DIA (Defense Intelligence Agency) ***(Declined Offer)***
2. Internal Revenue Service (IRS) ***(Declined Offer)***
3. NextGen
4. United Health Care
5. State of Georgia (Depart of Behavioral Health and Developmental Disabilities)
6. IBM
7. IHG (InterContinental Hotel Group)
8. Kaiser
9. MedAssets
10. Coventry Health Care
11. FirstData
12. Macy's Technology Systems
13. Georgia Tech
14. Total System Services, Inc.
15. Pinnacle
16. Fiserv
17. CGI
18. State of Georgia (Department of Community Health)
19. Board of Regents (Kennesaw State University)

| Business Name | Website |
|---|---|
| Assurant | https://assurant.taleo.net/careersection/10000/jobsearch.ftl?lang=en&src=CWS-10920 |
| Computer Sciences Corp | http://www.csc.com/careersus/flx/16177-job_opportunities |
| IBM Corp | https://jobs3.netmedia1.com/cp/search.jsp |
| GE | http://www.ge.com/careers/job_search.html |
| Turner Broadcasting | https://careers.timewarner.com/1033/ASP/TG/cim_home.asp?partnerid=391&siteid=36 |
| Hewlett Packard | https://hp.taleo.net/careersection/2/jobsearch.ftl;jsessionid=931243F97B55A3589034A4FD46C77983.JB_17489_17496?lang=en |
| TransUnion | http://www.transunion.com/corporate/aboutUs/careers/findAJob.page |
| Dunn&Bradstreet | http://www.dnb.com/US/about/careers/External/Frameset/external_frameset.asp |
| LexisNexis | https://reedelsevier.taleo.net/careersection/50/moresearch.ftl?lang=en |
| Coca-Cola | http://www.virtualvender.coca-cola.com/na_application.jsp |
| Coca-Cola Entps | http://enjoycareers.com/careers.aspx |
| Compuware | http://jobs-compuware.icims.com/jobs/intro?var=1 |
| Equifax | http://www.equifax.com/careers/opportunities/en_us |
| NASCO | https://careers-nasco.icims.com/jobs/intro |
| Home Depot | https://careers.peopleclick.com/careerscp/client_homedepot/external/search.do |
| Newell Rubbermaid | http://www.newellrubbermaid.com/Public/careers/jobopportunitiesusafrag.aspx |
| Southern Co. | http://www.southerncompany.com/careerinfo/iframe_professional_jobs.aspx |
| Total System | https://tsys.taleo.net/careersection/tsys.careersection.external.001/jobsearch.ftl?lang=en |
| Cox Enterprises | http://www.coxenterprises.com/coxcareer/eRecruit.asp |
| GA Pacific Corp | https://gp.recruitmax.com//main/careerportal/default.cfm?szUniqueCareerPortalID=28750195-0091-437c-b65f-a6b4d40b130c&szIsJobBoard=0 |
| SunTrust Banks | https://suntrust.taleo.net/careersection/2/moresearch.ftl?lang=en |
| Kimberly Clark | https://kimberlyclark.myvurv.com/MAIN/careerportal/default.cfm |
| Motorola Inc. | http://careers.motorolasolutions.com/moto.cfm?page=search_jobs |

| Business Name | Website |
|---|---|
| Travel Port | https://careers.travelport.com/OA_HTML/RF.jsp?function_id=13916&resp_id=23350&resp_appl_id=800&security_group_id=0&lang_code=US&params=uWuttR3y5l7gnL1E2f7htHe43-7Qt8WV6Qc4wAvKYulA9FRJ9h3yZayaxX4ZVCmk&oas=EFvVBroMh8R37lpGejx0EQ.. |
| Aetna Life Ins Co. | https://sjobs.brassring.com/1033/asp/tg/cim_home.asp?partnerid=25276&siteid=5012 |
| Atlanta Housing Authority | https://www2.ultirecruit.com/HOU1003/jobboard/ListJobs.aspx?__VT=ExtCan&CFID=14067030&CFTOKEN=14316759 |
| Avon Prod Inc. | https://avon.taleo.net/careersection/2/jobsearch.ftl?lang=en |
| Ceridian Employer Services Inc. | http://www.ceridian.com/corp/mycareer/1,6453,15653,00.html |
| Choicepoint Services Inc. | https://reedelsevier.taleo.net/careersection/50/moresearch.ftl?lang=en&jobfield=10901430233&radiusType=M&radius=1&organization=40101430233&location=18301430233 |
| Goodwill Ind of North Georgia | https://www1.apply2jobs.com/goodwillng/ProfExt/index.cfm?fuseaction=mExternal.showSearchInterface |
| International Paper Co. | http://www.internationalpaper.com/US/EN/Company/Careers/SearchPositions.html |
| INVESCO | https://sh.webhire.com/Public/79/indexD.htm |
| Manhattan Associates Inc. | http://www.manh.com/careers-manhattan-associates/job-postings-us |
| Panasonic | http://panasonic.taleo.net/careersection/external/jobsearch.ftl |
| Racetrac Petroleum Inc. | https://wfa.kronostm.com/index.jsp?seq=postingSearch&applicationName=RaceTracReqExt&locale=en_US |
| Radiant Sys Inc. | http://tbe.taleo.net/NA12/ats/careers/jobSearch.jsp?org=RADIANT&cws=1 |
| Scientific Games Operating Corp. | http://www.scigames.com/job-search.aspx |
| UNISYS Corporation | https://www.careers.unisys.com/psp/applicant/APPLICANT/UG_APPLICANT/c/HRS_HRAM.HRS_CE.GBL?Page=HRS_CE_HM_PRE&Action=A&SiteId=35 |
| Volt Services Grp. | http://jobs.volt.com/jobsearch/jobs.cfm |
| World Travel Partners | http://www.worldtravel.com/go/id/cbkw/ |
| Xerox Corp. | http://www.xeroxcareers.com/search-jobs/default.aspx |

## *Appendix B - User ID & Password List Template*

| Company | User ID | Password | Date |
|---|---|---|---|
| | | | |
| | | | |
| | | | |
| | | | |
| | | | |
| | | | |
| | | | |
| | | | |
| | | | |
| | | | |
| | | | |
| | | | |
| | | | |
| | | | |
| | | | |
| | | | |
| | | | |
| | | | |

| Business Name | Website |
|---|---|
| **Prudential Bank & Trust Co.** | https://pru.taleo.net/careersection/2/jobsearch.ftl?lang=en |
| **The Weather Channel** | http://www.weather.com/careers/postings.html |
| **Weyerhaeuser Company** | https://weyerhaeuser.taleo.net/careersection/10000/moresearch.ftl?lang=en |
| **InterContinental Hotels Group** | http://www.ihgplc.com/index.asp?pageid=430 |
| **Keane Inc.** | https://careers-keane.icims.com/jobs/intro |
| **Norfolk Southern Corp.** | https://www1.recruitingcenter.net/Clients/NS/PublicJobs/Canviewjobs.cfm? |
| **S1 Corp** | http://www.s1.com/AboutS1/US_Careers/UScareers.aspx |
| **Pepsi Cola Co.** | http://careers.pepsico.com/content/location/ |
| **Oracle** | https://irecruitment.oracle.com/OA_HTML/RF.jsp?function_id=1038712&resp_id=23350&resp_appl_id=800&security_group_id=0&lang_code=US&params=.1VlTZi5hyKHcE3E6mrZaB91phg4LLW-2ZXXJFOuaJdg-6ALqWl2AqDOwJZdQVEM&oas=xkLAYhtvwC8DqbHS4LXZvA.. |
| **ING Investment Management** | https://sjobs.brassring.com/EN/ASP/TG/cim_home.asp?partnerid=335&siteid=77 |
| **Technisource** | http://www.technisource.com/search/ |
| **Travelers Property Casualty** | http://hrjobs.stpaultravelers.com/psp/PSHR620/EMPLOYEE/HRMS/c/HRS_HRAM.HRS_CE.GBL?FolderPath=PORTAL_ROOT_OBJECT.HC_HRS_CE_GBL2&IsFolder=false&IgnoreParamTempl=FolderPath%2cIsFolder |
| **Automatic Data Processing** | http://www.adp-jobs.com/ |
| **EMS Tech** | http://www.ems-t.com/careers/careersoverview.aspx?id=125 |
| **EMC Corp.** | https://sjobs.brassring.com/1033/ASP/TG/cim_advsearch.asp?SID=^Id0a9ffW2KpuSu7hE9pVOq1mvWnAaFhJ_slp_rhc_9_slp_rhc_R954jUQGpUi_slp_rhc_lBuKr8y8BEadNiUzV&ref=1202011133926 |
| **Witness Systems** | http://verint.com/corporate/careers_list.cfm |
| **Agilent Technologies** | www.agilent.com |
| **Atlanta Journal & Constitution** | www.ajc.com |
| **Imaging Tech** | www.itserve.com |

| Business Name | Website |
|---|---|
| **Amazon.com, Inc.** | http://www.amazon.com/Search-Jobs-Careers/b/ref=amb_link_6001432_2?ie=UTF8&node=239362011&pf_rd_m=ATVPDKIKX0DER&pf_rd_s=center-2&pf_rd_r=15QXDNKCPP79ZR679QA7&pf_rd_t=101&pf_rd_p=434481001&pf_rd_i=203348011 |
| **American Express** | http://careers.americanexpress.com/?inav=footer_careers |
| **Apple Comp., Inc.** | http://www.apple.com |
| **Bank of America Corporation** | http://careers.bankofamerica.com/overview/overview.asp |
| **Bristol-Myers Squibb Company** | https://bms.taleo.net/careersection/ejs+external+career+site+w2fprofile+ques+v20090518/jobsearch.ftl?lang=en |
| **Campbell Soup Company** | http://www.campbellsoupcompany.apply2jobs.com/ProfExt/index.cfm?fuseaction=mExternal.showSearchInterface |
| **CBS Corporation** | https://sjobs.brassring.com/1033/ASP/TG/cim_advsearch.asp?partnerid=25084&siteid=5129&codes=CBS_Corp |
| **CIGNA Corporation** | http://careers.cigna.com/CIGNAPage.aspx?page=14 |
| **Cisco Systems, Inc.** | http://www.cisco.apply2jobs.com/index.cfm |
| **Citigroup Inc.** | https://citi.taleo.net/careersection/2/jobsearch.ftl?lang=en |
| **ConocoPhillips** | http://www.conocophillips.com/EN/careers/cop_careers/job_search/Pages/index.aspx |
| **Dell Inc.** | http://www.dell.com/content/topics/global.aspx/corp/careers/jobsearch/default?c=us&l=en&s=corp#top |
| **Delta Air Lines** | http://www.deltajobs.net/career_destinations.htm |
| **Eaton Corporation** | http://www.eaton.com/Eaton/OurCompany/Careers/NorthAmerica/ExperiencedCandidates/Careers/U.S.CareersSearch/index.htm |
| **Google Inc.** | http://www.google.com/intl/en/jobs/ |
| **Honeywell Int'l** | http://www.careersathoneywell.com/en/JobSearch.aspx |
| **IKON Office Solutions, Inc.** | https://www.ikonrecruiting.com/ikon/jobboard/searchjobs.aspx |
| **J. C. Penney Company, Inc.** | https://pshrwb200.jcpenney.com:7901/psc/zape/EMPLOYEE/HRMS/c/HRS_HRS.HRS_APP_SCHJOB.GBL?Page=HRS_APP_SCHJOB&Action=U& |
| **L-3 Communications Holdings, Inc.** | http://www.l-3com.com/careers/search-english.aspx |
| **Levi Strauss &Co** | http://www.levistrauss.com/careers/find-job?region=us |

| Business Name | Website |
| --- | --- |
| **Microsoft Corp.** | http://www.microsoft.com |
| **NCR Corp.** | http://www.ncr.com/about_ncr/careers/apply_now/search_us_opportunities_1.jsp |
| **NIKE, Inc.** | http://www.nikebiz.com/careers/us/ |
| **The Hartford Financial Services Group, Inc.** | https://thehartford.taleo.net/careersection/2/jobsearch.ftl?lang=en |
| **Unisys Corporation** | https://www.careers.unisys.com/psp/applicant/APPLICANT/UG_APPLICANT/c/HRS_HRAM.HRS_CE.GBL?Page=HRS_CE_HM_PRE&Action=A&SiteId=35 |
| **Vaco Technology** | http://www.vaco.com/search/jobs |
| **AT&T** | https://att.taleo.net/careersection/10161/moresearch.ftl |
| **Research In Motion Ltd.** | https://rim.taleo.net/careersection/americas/jobsearch.ftl?lang=en&location=4101430233 |
| **CIBER** | https://ciber.taleo.net/careersection/careersection/pro_orig/jobsearch.ftl |

# *Appendix E - Personal Unique Strengths*

### *My STRONGEST SKILLS*

1. I'm a Leader and Innovator
2. I am Results and Goals originated
3. I have the ability to get the job done
4. I need little to no supervision
5. I am a visionary thinker
6. I am a Self-starter and Self-motivated
7. I am very decisive, candid, straight-forward, and a very good listener
8. I am willing to take on more responsibility and is willing to step out in front and to take risk
9. I am able to get along with everyone and a Problem Solver

### *LEADERSHIP*

**Leadership** is the ability to inspire and motivate people to a worthwhile achievement.
**Leadership** is taking the person or company from where they are to where they ought to be.
**Leadership** is the ability to help people and organizations to surpass themselves.
**Leadership** is about influencing people to follow direction.
**Leaders** must be willing to lead to step out in front and to take risk.
**Leaders** are Life-Time Learners

**Invisible leadership**
Exercising the vision to change the traditional role from commander to coach, from manager to mentor, from director to delegator, from one who demands respect to one who facilitate self-respect.

### *MY STYLE*

I'm accountable, decisive and collaborative. I'm frank, candid, straightforward and a problem solver. And I listen to my staff or team.

1. I set as the goal the maximum capacity that people have!
2. I make myself a relentless architect of the possibilities of Human Being!
3. I settle for "NO" less!

### *MY WEAKNESSES*

1. I am impatient (speed is everything)
2. I determine my priorities quickly and expect others to have similar attitudes
3. I process issues quickly and want to move on, even when other people aren't ready to

I'm passionate about working in this Industry. I've been an asset to every employer I have ever had. I have worked with companies that had tough integration application development problems and needed a delivery solution. The solution I brought was leadership and a RESULT-ORIENTED method of getting the job done. And that would make me an even greater asset to YOU and [**firm's name**].

I think these are the most exciting times I have ever seen in this business. Companies that grow leaders and not managers will stand all alone at the top. I can help your organization meet these challenges. While my resume doesn't tell my whole story, it demonstrates that:

I'm good at what I do; I get results, because I have the capability of creating a path and direction focused on results and I'm a **Problem-Solver**. Also, I have the confidence and attitude to take on more responsibility to lead an organization to the next level.

I will bring a good perspective to this position because I've been a doer, as well as a leader. The people who have worked with and for me have always respected my judgment and fair play, because they know I have integrity and a very good understanding of what needs to be done.

And I have a terrific business sense. I'm great at re-inventing myself; you must re-invent yourself before the market-place re-invents you out of a career. I have a knack of developing a good chemistry with upper management, staff, customers and clients. I have an absolute commitment to the organization success.

I also believe in continuous improvement and learning. I believe in "ONE MINUTE EXECLLENCE"! You make a decision to be the best, then it's done, and then you work to continue being the best.

I'm a team-player who can roll up his sleeves and help out wherever needed. I can work alone or in a team environment and I'm truly excited about the opportunity of working for [**firm's name**].

## *Appendix G - Interviewing Questions*

1. What kind of person are you looking for to fill this position? What is your ideal job candidate like?

2. What are the day-to-day responsibilities of the position?

3. What qualities do you appreciate most in a member of your staff? What do you appreciate least?

4. What are this job's priorities for the first few months?

5. When I'm hired, what would my first project be?

6. What are the biggest challenges that you are facing in this department?

7. What are the most important problems that you'd like the person in this job to solve?

8. What things make it attractive to be an employee of your company?

9. Describe your leadership style?

10. Do you have any other questions or concerns about my ability that you are not comfortable with to determine that I'm the right person for the position?

11. When will a decision be made about the person hired?

## DARNELL CLARKE, MBA, PMP®

### EXECUTIVE PROFILE

Dynamic, hands-on leader with a strong understanding of business execution and achievement of business metrics, predictable and accurate forecasting, and program management

### NOTABLE CONTRIBUTIONS

- Led efforts with Director, other Operations Managers, and P&L Leaders execute the systems engineering and DE Operations visions and strategies to improve the operating performance of the business.
- Instituted a program management office (PMO) processes including the coordination of key reviews (Deep Dives and Staff Reviews) prioritizing and defining enhancements, directing resources as needed to accomplish the vision/strategy and the communication of results / progress

### PROFESSIONAL EXPERIENCE

*General Electric Company– Digital Energy, Atlanta, Georgia*

**Technology Operations Manager**, 02/2011 – Present

Responsible for establishing a regular operational rhythm that increases process rigor to drive overall productivity. Monitor progress through monthly operational and deep dive reviews. I track performance in key areas like budget, EHS, Green Belt and Say-Do's to make sure GE is accountable for what we say and do. Managing $14 million budget and 4 program managers.

*TRINITY HEALTH, Farmington Hills, Michigan*

**Enterprise Sr. Manager**, 01/2009 – 12/2010

Responsible for Trinity's strategy, planning, designing, and implementation of the ambulatory (physician office) business for the firm. Responsible for the multi-source data warehouse which is fed from the Revenue Systems (HealthQuest), from a home-grown Cost Accounting System and from the Hospital-Based Clinical System (Cerner), and from our Physician Office System (NextGen). Managed $7 million budget and 35 employees and contractors/vendors.

*GEORGIA TECHNOLOGY AUTHORITY, Atlanta, Georgia*
**Director, IT Strategic Planning**, 05/2007 – 12/2008
Responsible for State agencies in Georgia spend $684.1 million; including strategic planning, governance, policies and standards, enterprise portfolio management, performance measures, review and approval of agency requests for technology to facilitate better decision making.

**EDUCATION**

University of Georgia, Athens, Georgia
MBA, Business Administration

Wayne State University, Detroit, Michigan
BA, Computer Science

1. "**Think & Grow Rich**" by Napoleon Hill
2. "**Now Discover your Strengths**" and "**StandOut**" by Marcus Buckingham
3. "**Occupational Outlook Handbook**" and "**Career Guide to Industries**" by U.S. Bureau of Labor Statistics (http://www.bls.gov/oco/)
4. "**The Dream Giver**" by Bruce Wilkinson
5. "**Financial Peace Revisited**" and "**The Total Money Makeover**" by Dave Ramsey
6. "**The Great Boom Ahead, The Roaring 2000, The Next Great Bubble Boom, The Great Depression Ahead, and The Great Crash Ahead**" by Harry S. Dent
7. "**The Wealth of Nations**" by Adam Smith
8. "**The General Theory of Employment, Interest, and Money**" by John Maynard Keynes